A Journey Through
Illness and Addiction

DIANA LEE

Silently Said
Copyright © 2022 by Diana Lee

All rights reserved. No part of this publication may be reproduced, distributed, or transmitted in any form or by any means, including photocopying, recording, or other electronic or mechanical methods, without the prior written permission of the author, except in the case of brief quotations embodied in critical reviews and certain other non-commercial uses permitted by copyright law.

Tellwell Talent
www.tellwell.ca

ISBN
978-0-2288-7532-1 (Hardcover)
978-0-2288-1184-8 (Paperback)
978-0-2288-1185-5 (eBook)

Preface

This book has taken as many years to write as years I've lived. The passion I feel for writing collided with the fact that I was gifted a less than ordinary life. I didn't know this gift existed when I was a child but certainly felt connected to the written word. Writing provided a release I had never experienced. Writing has become my favourite blanket, taking the frost out of an icy story.

This book danced with publication several times, and I held it back each time concerned about outing myself and the way people would perceive me. There was also the debilitating fear and doubt. However, writing this book has been gloriously full of life lessons that need not be justified but simply laid before you as an offering. Take what you feel resonates, leave what does not. I ask for your patience as you weave along the path of lessons well-learned and well-earned.

Dedication

To my dearest mother and sister: Your sacrifices did not go unnoticed. It is the reason this book exists. Your lives ignited my purpose. There is always purpose to the pain. Through this journey I learned to grow. Thank you.

To my family: The patience you showed has not gone unnoticed. Your shoulders were always there to carry my tears as I walked myself through my grief. You always gave my heart and soul a place to feel safe and rest, and I am profoundly grateful.

To Lindsay, my grade school friend that I have had the honour of walking through life with: Thank you for being a steadfast friend; for your devotion that comes from a lifetime of understanding, compassion, empathy and friendship.

Thank you to my dearest friend, Carrie. You are a shining example of a true and trusted friend. I am ever grateful to travel our growth journey together.

To my Auntie Betty: Thank you for helping me learn to stand on my own and for your belief in me.

I must thank two of my English teachers from school: my Grade 8 teacher, Ms. Scott, and my grades 10–12 English teacher, Mr. Link. Both saw my potential as a writer and helped me develop my gift.

Lastly, to my brothers: The ride was rough, but we became stronger together. I couldn't ask for better siblings to ride the ups and downs with. I am grateful for the bond this created between us and where the journey has taken us. Strangely, I would not change a thing.

I love you all.

Prologue

Mom falls to the floor, tears flowing as heavily as the water that is running wildly from the faucet. Confused, I crawl back up to the sink, but the pants around my ankles make it harder as try to turn the water off myself. Panicked, I can't. The tap won't budge. It's stuck wide open. My small hands grasp the cold faucet, but it's slippery. Water keeps flowing and fills the sink; pipes unable to keep up. Water rushes over the sink's edge, cascading down, quickly soaking the floor and forcing me off the counter as I slip in the wet mess.

Mom is sobbing on the floor. She had tried, unsuccessfully, to turn it off for me. Scared and scathed, I fold my tiny four-year-old body into my mother's shaky rail-like arms. Her clutch is rigid, not soft and smooth; I am met with her tight, stiff embrace. I wedge my small frame into her and we cry. I look up to her for answers knowing she cannot talk well anymore; in fact, I don't recall a time when she ever did. I need to know our house will not fill with water, that we will not drown. Instead, all I see behind those haunting steel blue eyes is unbridled fear. I sense then that there is more to Mom's tears, *But what?* I wonder. Much of the time I sense things I cannot find words for; they are just beyond my language, but I know there is something more going on. When your mother is non-verbal, you must find a way to communicate. Ours is through facial expressions and those eyes.

My dad has told us Mom is sick with a nameless disease. I know it's not a cold or a flu, and her tummy doesn't hurt. I remember the day we picked up her wheelchair. I sat between Mom and Dad in the doctor's office as they discussed her walking issues. When we brought it home, us kids made the best out of it. Chris made us all laugh by learning to pop a wheelie! Even the sombre look on our parents' faces broke into amazement at Chris's trick! That was us, always trying to turn the mood around.

Now, Mom's words are broken and few, mostly "No" or "Yes." Her body is stiff, movements forced like the robots on *Star Wars*. A few relatives told me that this nameless mystery illness appeared when Mom was pregnant with my sister, Kimberley. Allegedly, our father was in denial so there were no other visits to the doctor's office except for her check-ups during her pregnancy. When Kim was fifteen months old and Mom was pregnant with me, the symptoms could no longer be ignored. Her walking slowed to a shuffle, so much so that Dad often remarked that she should pick up her feet. Obviously, she could not. Her movements and her memory slowed. I'm not sure how many times Dad scolded Mom for leaving food cooking on the stove while she was outside, but she loved the outdoors and was not much of a cook or housekeeper. Soon everyone knew something was wrong, but what?

According to my brothers, I came into this world in the middle of a cold, snowy March night right on the cusp of winter meeting spring. All the kids were awoken from their warm sleepy slumber to pile onto the cold, hard pleather seats of the family station wagon and drive Mom to the hospital. Labour and delivery was quick and painful. Shortly after having me, Mom became incapable of caring for her four young children.

The sound of the squeaky front door, barely audible amongst the thrashing water, perks my ears. The slam confirms my guess: My oldest brother, Aaron, walks into the house just in the nick of time! I free myself from my mother's clutch and yell for help. He races up the stairs, blows past me to the sink, my panicked words chasing him. With the quick ease of a ten-year-old, Aaron turns the tap off.

Finally, everything seems to be under control. Everything except for Mom. As she slumps on the soaking wet mint green linoleum, her milky white hands cover her tear-streaked face, but her long, bony fingers hide little. I like her fingers, long and elegant, each knuckle defined yet dainty; I secretly hope mine look like hers one day. She is soaked, still crying. I don't understand; the water is off and the house no longer in danger. I tilt my head and wrinkle my nose in confusion. I ponder her sadness and chastise myself for not being able to turn the tap off, for scaring my mother and upsetting her. Her tears become wails as guilt rises inside me. *This is my fault*, I tell myself. Yet there is a sense inside me that lurks beyond the guilt and shame. Inside my young mind rests a quiet knowing, a guidepost to point my little soul. *But where?* I ask myself. I am confused by this lure of senses, yet they soothe me. Curious, I follow my intuition and allow myself to explore. Intuitively, I reach inside my young soul and am surprised at what I find: a voice that says *This is not about you.*

Sitting on the floor, she is now at eye level with me. I try to pull her hands away from her face to look at her, but they seem cemented in place, a result of stubbornness or illness, I can't decide.

"Mommy, Mommy," I urge her eyes to join mine. "Mommy, it's okay; Aaron got the water off. The house isn't going to flood. Everything is okay."

I am met with silence while mom tightens her eyelids. I sense her fear and try once more to soften her.

"Mommy, I know I did a bad thing and that I scared you. I am sorry. I won't do it again, Mommy. Okay? I was scared, too, but everything is okay now. I'll clean up the mess, I promise."

My soothing words go unnoticed, which is when I realize they are actually calming me. This is when the role reversal happened, albeit subconsciously. Child becomes parent. Parent, child. Nurturing became my nature. And as hard as it must have been for my mother, we cared for her.

Chapter 1

Kindergarten Kid

I loved kindergarten. The very thought of joining my brothers and sister on the bus without Mom and Dad excited me! I dreamt of riding that bus every time it came into our farmyard. Sometimes I would wait for the bus outside in the morning with my siblings. That big yellow taxi would pull in and whisk them all away, and I wanted nothing more than to be whisked away too. In late afternoon, I would find the family dog, Rex, sitting on the wooden patio table, waiting for the bus. Sometimes I would join him. We had lots of pets: our dog Rex, cats Newie and Cougar, and a few rabbits named Midnight and Henry Kelsey. When I was younger we had pigs, but now we had goats, turkeys and chickens. Even though the days without my siblings were long, I kept company with my animal friends except for the turkeys; they were mean!

I was five years old when I started kindergarten in September 1983. I was so excited the night before that I could hardly sleep! My mom's caregiver, Dean (who was a lady, which was confusing because I thought it was a boy's name), packed up my lunch in my *Gremlins* lunch kit. I gazed at it in our fridge beside the rest of them. *It's finally my turn!*

"Dad, I'm going to go to bed now. Maybe if I sleep, morning will get here faster!" I announced to my father, who was sitting in the living room watching *Dallas,* Mom in her wheelchair.

They both looked in my direction, and Dad replied, "Diana, it's only 7:00 p.m. Maybe you want to come watch TV with your mom and me for a bit, then go to bed?"

I didn't know how to tell time, but I felt it moved too slowly.

"If I go to bed now, Dad, it will be my first day of school when I wake up!"

The commercial break was over, and my dad went back to his show so I strolled off to my bedroom. I sat on the edge of the twin captain bed I shared with my sister and started to change into my pajamas.

"Diana, what are you doing? It's too early for bed!" Kimberley said as she walked in.

Having just been told this by Dad, I decided to ignore her as I finished pulling my nightie over my head. Kim must have decided she didn't care anymore and pulled out some Barbie from our cardboard toybox underneath the staircase in our bedroom. I found my clothes for school, a pair of jeans and a rainbow-coloured top with ruffles on the shoulders—and put them atop our shared white dresser. Dean had ordered our new school clothes from the Sears catalogue, and they had come in the mail a few days before school. Rarely did I get new clothes, so this made my excitement grow. Now that I was ready for bed, I turned our bedroom light off. Kim complained but soon moved her Barbies to the staircase beside our bedroom. The door was left open because neither Kim nor I liked the dark. Dad usually kept a light on in the kitchen which we could see from our bedroom.

As I laid awake too excited to sleep, I got an idea. *I want to sleep with my lunchkit tonight!* So, I trotted out of my bedroom and crept into the kitchen. I ever so quietly opened our cream-coloured fridge and pulled out my lunchkit from the row. As I raced back to my bedroom with the goods in hand, Kim met me at our bedroom doorway.

"Why do you have your lunchkit? That's for tomorrow," she scolded.

I walked past her, not caring what she thought. I tucked myself back into bed, this time my lunchkit nestled against my chest, arms clutching it tightly. It wasn't as cuddly as my stuffed animals, but I was unphased.

"Diana, you know Dad's going to see it when he comes to tuck you in, don't you?"

Realizing she was right, I slipped the lunchkit lower under my blankets.

"Yeah, well just don't tell him," I replied.

I could not sleep. I laid awake for what felt like hours, but sleep would not come. I finally got up when I figured it must be morning and climbed into my school clothes. Did I notice it was dark outside? I did not. I picked up my lunchkit and went to find dad.

"Dad, I'm ready for school now," I announced, standing in front of him as he laid on the couch watching TV.

"Diana, it's 9:00 p.m.," Dad said as he sat up. "Go put your lunchkit back in the fridge, put your pajamas back on and go to bed please."

When dad directed, I listened, mostly.

I delivered my lunchkit back to the fridge where it assumed its position beside the others. When I got back to my bedroom, Kim was in bed too. I decided that if I couldn't sleep with my lunchkit, I would at least sleep in my clothes so that when I got up, I would be ready! Kim chided me once more, but I didn't care. Nothing could deflate my excitement for my first day of school not even the idea of getting heck!

When the bus pulled up the next day, I assumed my usual position beside my siblings, but this time I experienced riding it! It was thrilling! Some teenagers, who I was scared of, wanted me to come sit with them. They said I looked like a cabbage patch kid! I sat in the front instead. The bus pulled up to the old brick school with a large cement staircase first, which is the school I attended. I loved that staircase, but the one inside the building was far grander. I longed to walk up that wooden staircase, but the upstairs was reserved for the older grades, the staffroom and the giant recess bell. This brick school was home to kindergarten to Grade 3 and lots of bats! That's right, bats! Sometimes they flapped their way into our classroom, which was scary, but the janitor took care of them, sometimes with a badminton racket.

My kindergarten teacher was Mrs. Smith, and she asked that the students find their name on their desks. I couldn't read but knew my name started with "D," and I surprised myself when I was praised for taking the correct seat. My chances were better than most at finding my name as their was another 'Diana" in my class. The day strolled along nicely with story time, nap time (which I did not feel was necessary), lunch and recess. Lots of my Story Hour friends were there, so I knew most of my class. At the end of the day, our teacher announced that we had some "homework" to do tonight! I had heard my siblings complain of homework, but the idea that I would be just like them and have my very own homework to do had me beaming!

"Now class, tonight you have a special assignment," Mrs. Smith announced. "Since we were talking about stars today, when it's dark tonight, look outside to the north. You will find a constellation that looks like this."

She held up a picture of some stars, and I didn't see anything special about them.

"This is the Big Dipper; it's made up of seven stars," she said as she pointed to them to show us the shape.

She then gave us each a sheet of paper with the Big Dipper on it. Armed with homework in my backpack, I proudly march onto the big yellow bus once again. I see Kim is already on and I scoot over to sit with her. The ride feels far too quick as we arrive home.

I bust through the front door to find Dean in the dining room and Mom in the living room watching *Another World*.

"Where's Dad?" I asked, scanning the room.

"He's in the shop. He will be taking me home soon. Supper will be ready at 5:00, but you can have a small snack if you want," Dean said, handing me two of her world famous chocolate chip oatmeal cookies!

Silently Said

The perfect end to the perfect day.

My siblings offered to help me with my homework once it was dark enough out. Aaron even said we may have to stay up a bit later to make sure we would see it. Dad took Dean home before supper, and we waited for him to come back before we ate, but it was already 6:00 p.m. and we usually ate around 5:00 p.m. With hungry tummies, we decided to eat; roasted chicken with mashed potatoes, gravy and corn. We had mashed potatoes for every meal, and I secretly wished we could have something else. Since Mom could not feed herself any longer, we mashed up her food and fed it to her. Aaron or Chris usually took the lead on this, mixing in a bit of water so the food would go down easier. It was Chris's turn to feed her, and he prepped the food syringe, making sure it was clean, and sucked up the runny potatoes and gravy. It looked gross, but Mom didn't complain; she couldn't really. We knew when she was full as she would turn her head away when we brought food to her mouth. Today, however, she was hungry and finished her plate.

Dad was still not home after we'd finished, so we packed up the food and put it in the fridge. Kim and I were tasked with making lunches; two ham sandwiches with mustard (butter for Aaron, no butter for Chris) and a bologna sandwich each for Kim and me. We cleaned out the lunch kits and repacked them, placing them back in the fridge for morning.

We then converged in the living room to keep Mom company and watch some TV until it got dark outside. Mom was in her wheelchair, but we always placed her walker, which she still could use some, close by in the event she wanted to get up. Aaron and Chris announced at 8:30 p.m. that it was dark enough to see the Big Dipper, so us four kids raced upstairs to the boys' bedroom, which faced the north. Chris had told us there was talk of switching the house around and that Kim and I would come upstairs. Mom and Dad would be downstairs as Mom couldn't make it up the stairs well anymore. Apparently, Dad was planning on adding onto the farmhouse, which excited both Kim and me. I longed to have the boys bedroom, but I would paint it a different colour than blue if Dad let me.

I showed them the picture my teacher had given me, and we peered out the window in search of the Big Dipper. All I had to do was tell the teacher that we did it; I didn't have to write anything about it, which was good considering I couldn't write yet.

"There it is!" Aaron announced.

Chris claimed to see it, too, but I thought they were full of it.

"No way! I don't see it, it's not here," I announced.

"Yes, it is Diana," the boys said in unison. "Right there," they whispered, pointing.

I tried my level best, but there was no way I could see what they saw. There were so many stars, and it was too dark. I was an overly emotional child at times, and this situation stressed me out.

"Diana, just look this way. See?" Chris moved my head into position to see the constellation.

I faintly heard our mother making sounds, trying to holler for us downstairs, but I couldn't reply until I got this homework assignment done. We all continued to look as Mom's noises became louder. Not being able to speak many words, she was left with a series of moans and grunts. None of us budged from our post until we heard a crash.

We raced to the staircase beside the boys' bedroom where we found our mother laying on her back, crying.

"She fell down the stairs!" Aaron exclaimed. "Chris, call Dad at the bar."

Most of our father's nights were spent at the local bar. We took care of our mother and became so good at it that we only called Dad at the bar if there was an emergency. With blood pouring from Mom's elbow, we knew this was one of those situations.

Chris hung up the phone after speaking with Dad.

"Yeah, he's at the bar. He will be home soon," he said.

Aaron looked at us all and formulated a plan.

"Chris, help me get Mom up. Kim, get Mom's wheelchair. Diana, find the bandages and iodine."

Like the good soldiers we were, each of us commanded our post and did what we could to help. Once Mom was safely back in her chair, the boys cleaned up her wound and put a bandage on. Kim was scared and stayed back, but I held Mom's hand and wiped her tears away with some toilet paper. We moved Mom to her bedroom where it took all four of us to get her into her bed. We snuggled up beside her and waited for Dad to come home. Sadly, that wasn't until the early hours of the morning.

Chapter 2

Words and Their Influence

In the early 1980s, telephones were still attached to cords which were attached to walls, unlike today where they're attached to people. Ours was on a special table made for telephones; where the phone, pens, paper and phonebook sat. The other side was lower, with a chair connected to the table. An ingenious idea, really; you could sit and chat and be completely comfortable. Cords were short but conversations were not.

We had a pinkish rotary dial—you know the type; if your phone number started with a 9, which ours did, you had to wait those few extra seconds before moving to the next digit—not the push-button one some of my friends had. Making a phone call meant taking your time to dial.

Our line, like many in rural Saskatchewan, was a party line. This meant that when you picked up the phone, there could be someone having a gossip session about the latest happenings on *Another World* or perhaps a farmer ordering parts for his broken-down combine from the dealership in Kindersley. There was also a special ring for you so you didn't answer all the rings that came through.

We shared our party line with the neighbours, Frank and Sally, who lived to the southeast of our farm. I could see their yard from our south and east windows. Sally was quite the chatter, and the chances of getting a free line to dial out on were few and far between, which was a source of never-ending frustration for my dad.

I wasn't allowed to use the phone. If someone was calling and no one else was in the house, I still did not answer. Occasionally, I would be allowed speak with my grandma on the phone, but that didn't happen often because she lived close by in a small village named Plenty. Since we spent much time at her home, we didn't need to call. At the age of four, the phone was simply a grown-up tool for grown-up conversations or in case of emergency.

I used to enjoy the more practical things such as dinky cars, Barbie dolls and climbing trees. I also pretended to be a pioneer on the old wagon, which dad had placed the farm fuel tank on. I also liked to pretend I was a farmer from yesteryear, climbing all over the old, rusty thrashing machine down by the dugout. Dusk 'til dawn, we were outside. I spent many afternoons playing dinky cars with my siblings, although Aaron seemed far too mature for this game. We would go out to a patch of unplanted tilled-up garden and make communities and roads for our little cars and tractors to travel. Usually, Chris would grab the old, splintered hoe from the garage and move the larger clumps of gumbo soil out of the way so the small toys could smoothly manoeuvre through our little community of make-believe. The hoe served a double-purpose as it also allowed us to create mounds, which we pretended were the houses of our friends.

When nature wouldn't co-operate, we moved our favourite childhood game indoors, usually to the boys' bedroom. They had flooring that mimicked roads and fields. Three-inch brown squares outlined by one-inch white lines meant we could use the cultivators or seeder in the brown "soil," as it was the wrong colour for pretending it was a growing or mature crop. We didn't have any dirt houses, so we stacked my *Archie* comic books one on top of the other to create the frame of a house.

Chris always kept the best dinky cars and tractors for himself, but he was good about sharing the old ones. Brothers! Sometimes Kim and I would put up a stink when he kept all the shiny new equipment and we were left with the dirty old ones, but we knew if we wanted to play with the nice ones one day we had better talk nicely to him!

There were times he was generous and allowed us to play with his nicer toys. He always took good care of them, carefully shining them up and displaying them proudly in his room. I liked how that looked and tried to copy him by organizing my stuffed animals on my bed in some sort of order. I looked up to him. He, like Aaron, protected me.

On one rainy, dreary afternoon, the three of us were playing upstairs when Chris, a growing eight-year-old who always seemed to be hungry, determined we should have a snack. Snack time in our house was almost unheard of. Unless permitted, we did not eat outside the allotted breakfast, lunch, after school or supper times. It was too early for our 3:00 o'clock snack but Chris said he could not wait. My siblings constantly made me sneak downstairs to the cereal cupboard, quickly and quietly open it, stick my hands in the box of cereal and bring it back to them.

"Come on, Diana. You know if you get caught Dad won't punish you like he would me," Chris pleaded.

It was compelling, mostly because it was true, but I still felt the butterflies of apprehension dancing in my belly.

"I don't know, Chris; Dad is usually pretty mean if we don't ask first."

"You know he will say no if you ask! How about you put one fistful in your mouth and then carry two up in your hands for Kim and I? That way we all get the same amount. Fair?"

Chris was big on fair, but fair to Chris meant him getting a little more.

"Will you let me play with your new John Deere tractor?" I asked.

This was going to be my leverage, the deal breaker. I didn't mind risking trouble as long as I got to play with that sleek, shiny rich green John Deere tractor! If I was caught, I could bat my hazel eyes and bank on the fact that I was Daddy's little girl even though the title came with few perks.

In the life of a farmer, a rainy day triggers one of two things: appreciation for a break or time to fix machinery in the Quonset. Rarely would you get both. Dad chose to take a break that day and was downstairs, which meant when Chris set me on mission cereal snack, I knew it was risky.

I carefully manoeuvred down the old staircase, making sure my light frame did not cause a stair to creek. The slender, wooden stairs were steep and cool to the touch. If so much as one squeak peeped out of these stairs, I could be caught. I heard some faint chatter, but it was not until I was at the bottom of the staircase and peeked around the corner that I realized Dad was on the phone. The cereal cupboard was directly beside the phone, so I slowly backed up to the steps and hunkered down to wait. I knew he could really talk if he got into a story, so I figured I might as well sit and listen until the coast was clear.

"She is using a wheelchair more now. Just can't take much walking anymore. Her balance is off, so if she tries to, she has to use her walker. It's hard in this house, with the bathroom and our bedroom being upstairs. We are thinking of doing an addition to the house. The doctors still don't have a diagnosis other than something with the central nervous system. They're talking about taking her to Saskatoon to study her for a couple of weeks. Not sure when, but the neurologists want to study this disease, whatever it is, a little closer. They don't know anyone else with the same symptoms. Right now, there isn't much hope. We can't even get a name for the illness out of these doctors! It would seem everyone is just as baffled as me. All I know is this isn't good and she will never recover. How bad it's going to get is hard to say, but my guess is really bad."

Conversations such as these were not uncommon in our home. It seemed Dad had limited information, as did the doctors.

Where's Mom? I wondered. Was she sitting in the living room listening to this? Maybe she was lying down, which was my secret hope, as my mission may have been compromised if she was in the living room and turned her head when I went for the cereal. Honestly, what I should have been thinking of were my mother's feelings and how it felt to be the constant centre of sad and depressing conversations about her ailing health. People usually talked about her like she wasn't in the room because she couldn't add to the conversation other than to slam her hand in protest and mumble "No." I noticed that her wedding band was bent flat, no longer a nice round circle as it had been when she married our father in 1971, from years of slamming her hands on the table attached to her wheelchair. It took a toll on both the ring and her body.

"You know this is hard on us all. She is only thirty, and having those four kids may be too hard on her. Maybe we shouldn't have had the last one. If we didn't, chances are she wouldn't have gotten sick."

The words slapped against my heart. I had never thought that having me would have made Mom sick. The guilt and shame hit full force, weighing my four-year-old body down. Mom's illness was my fault. I took away motherhood from her and took away my siblings' mom.

Although Dad carried on his conversation for a while longer, I had stopped listening. The stairs had become uncomfortable as did my feet against the white tiled floors. I wasn't sure what to do. I couldn't share this news with anyone. *Do I really need to get the cereal?* I thought. I looked over my right shoulder to see Chris and Kimberley eagerly waiting. Frustrated, I flapped my hands, mimicking Dad's conversation.

Chapter 3

Peavey Mart Santa

Peavey Mart was a forty-minute drive away, in Kindersley. It was my dad's one-stop shop: wrenches, parts, baby chicks, work and kids' clothes, candy bars and toys could all be found under the red sign. If time permitted, he would make what felt like twenty laps around that store, examine what each isle contained while leafing through the flyer full of sales, and pick up whatever he needed for the farm.

The wind was blowing hard when Dad summoned us into the 1974 Chevy Caprice station wagon. The pleather seats froze my bottom, so I was careful to place my mitts down on my seat before sitting down. I would then retract my hands into my winter coat for warmth, hoping the heat would kick in quickly. Aaron got the coveted front seat when Mom was not along. Quiet jealousy seethed in Kimberley and I, but Chris would pipe up, "I get the front on the way home!" With the wave of a hand, Dad would acknowledge Chris's comment. The ranks were clearly drawn between those two. We also knew we took orders from Dad, Mom's caregiver or Aaron. The purpose of that coveted front seat was clearly respect and rank, which is why Kim and I kept quiet. The younger you were, the further down the ranks you sat. You couldn't get further than my position; I had zero authority and was last in line.

It wasn't often we went to Kindersley midweek with Dad. We usually found out when we got off the school bus that Dad had gone to Kindersley and would arrive back in time to take Dean home. It was Christmas break, and Dean was there for the day, so Dad decided we could all go along.

Dad pulled up to the front of the store in search for a parking spot. The lot was pretty full for a Wednesday afternoon, and we all wondered why. Dad led our clan into the store, but not before setting out the ground rules.

"Don't ask for anything, you hear? We can't afford it. Plus, it's almost Christmas, and if you've been good, you'll have something new soon enough."

I once asked my dad about God, and he said, "God keeps two stacks of hay for each person. If your good stack of hay is bigger than your bad stack of hay when you die, you get into heaven." I applied the same principle to Santa, so I didn't dare breathe my daydreams of a new Barbie into words, to my dad, for fear the "haystack of good" I had piled up over the year would be immediately moved over to the bad.

None of us knew the parking lot was plumb full because a special visitor was in town: Santa! He was sitting on a big red chair in the corner near the exit sign. Kids were lined up well down the aisle, some standing alone, others with their parents. I continued to follow in step with my family, but my eyes were firmly set on this man with flushed cheeks and a beard as white as snow. His hair was thin but his belly was not. A mixture of excitement and fear danced in my belly, creating a steady nervous gurgle. I thought I may throw up. My thoughts were forced back to reality when I ran into Kim when she stopped.

"Hey, watch it!" Kim chided.

Embarrassed and annoyed, I said, "Sorry! Not like I hurt you!"

Dad was pulling out his flyer, list and pen, and he shot us both a glare. We were quiet immediately.

"Okay, you guys can all go look at the toys if you want. I have lots of things to pick up today. If you want to sit on Santa's lap, that's fine, but I don't want to be waiting on you when I'm ready to leave! When I'm done, I'll look in the toy section or the line for Santa. Don't leave the store."

With that, dad grabbed his cart and walked away. Chris and Aaron didn't wait to hear mine and Kim's plans, they went straight to the toy section. Aaron liked trains, and Chris liked building models of vehicles, so I was sure they were in the boring section.

"Let's go sit on Santa's lap, Kim! Please come with me!" I begged.

"But I want to look at all the toys, Diana," Kim said, looking towards the big display of Barbies and Barbie accessories.

"I do, too, Kim, but I don't know how long Dad will be here, and the only way we will get anything from those shelves is to ask Santa! Remember, Dad told us he has no money and our only chance to get something is to ask Santa."

"Okay, how about this:" Kim reasoned. "We go look at the toys together, then you go talk to Santa and tell him what we both want. I'm going to stay in the toy aisle. I don't want to go up and talk to him."

Kim was not one to talk to anyone besides me. I often observed her interactions with people, including our father, and it was apparent she was not a talker. I was a talker and usually did enough of it for the two of us anyway.

"If we spend some time in the toy aisle together, we can figure out exactly what we want, then you can go tell Santa."

Kim pleaded a good case and I knew it, so I agreed.

The aisles were full of colourful options, and every toy imaginable was at my fingertips. My hands glided over the Easy-Bake Oven box, dreaming of what Kim and I could bake. Kim and I sized up the section then found the boys exactly where I thought they'd be. Aaron was looking at trains and electrical boards while Chris stared at the model kits and remote-control vehicles.

"Do you guys want me to ask for anything from Santa for you? I'm going to stand in line."

The boys exchanged looks I didn't understand.

"Um, no thanks," Chris responded, and they both went back to their respective posts.

"Their loss," I muttered to Kim as we rounded back to the toys that held our hearts. "I want this Barbie with the big gown and tiara," I said, lifting the Barbie off the shelf and showing Kim.

"Yes!" Kim exclaimed. "It's so hard to choose! I don't want Santa to say no!"

"What do you mean?" I said, putting down the Barbie I had been admiring. "Do you think my good haystack isn't big enough to ask for a present?"

Kim's look met me with the fear I felt jumping around inside me. "I don't know. Why do you think I don't want to go up there!" she stated.

Realizing Santa might say "No," I decided to rethink this plan. I examined the line-up and noticed that the children who were on Santa's lap looked happy—no tears and no anger—so I took my place at the end of the winding line-up of nervous and excited children.

As the line inched closer to Santa, the jumping feeling in my tummy changed to a gurgle. Plus, I needed to pee. Leaving the line wasn't an option, so I crossed my legs and wished Kim would come stand with me so I could have gone to the washroom. I looked back at my sister, who was peering around the corner of the toy section at me. I motioned her over, but she wouldn't budge. I didn't know how to motion that I had to pee without announcing it to the line-up, so I just settled on other thoughts instead. I liked to believe she was proud of me and my bravery for asking for what we both wanted. This was the start of a long, silently said understanding that I would speak for her.

Finally, Santa called for the next child in line, and I excitedly climbed up on his big knee! This wasn't like sitting on my dad's boney knees, not at all! Santa's knee was much softer, kind of like sitting on a pillow. I looked Santa straight in the eye, grinning brightly and showing the gap between my front teeth. Santa smiled back.

"Well, little one, what would you like for Christmas?" Santa said with a jolly laugh.

"Santa, I want you to know I'm on the good list," I stated very matter-of-factly.

"Oh yes, I know. I had my elf check when you were waiting in line. He said you've been very good."

I looked towards the elf and am comforted, but when I looked past him, I saw my dad in line to pay for his items, smiling as he watched me. My brothers and sister had joined him, and they were all whispering and chattering about me and Santa.

"Now, what is it you would like for Christmas?" Santa said, bringing me back to our conversation.

My tummy started to flip around again at the thought of telling Santa what I wanted.

"Well, I'd like two Barbies dressed in gowns, please! Any gown, I don't care."

Santa, looking a little surprised, took my shoulders and pushed me back to have a better look at me.

"But why on earth would you want Barbie dolls when you're a little boy? Little boys should be asking for things like tractors and cars, not Barbie dolls!"

The words thumped against my little heart hard.

"What do you mean, Santa? I'm a little girl," I said.

Looking down at my brown corduroy pants and light blue jacket, I knew what he meant. Dad kept my hair short even though I had begged him to let me grow it out so I could have braids and ponytails. He said I would have this haircut until I could manage my own hair.

"Oh, you're a girl," Santa said, clearing his throat. "Well, little girl, it's mighty greedy to ask for two Barbies. Most good little girls ask for only one."

I was torn by the insult, yet still aware of the power he held.

"Well, Santa," I said in my best good girl voice, "I asked for two because my sister was too shy to come sit on your lap."

I pointed her out in the line-up, and he seemed to soften.

"Oh, she is too scared to meet Santa? There is nothing to be scared of, right?"

I smiled in agreement, but I knew I would never sit on Santa's lap again, not after he called me a boy!

"What's your sister's name?" Santa inquired. "Kimberley. She is six, I'm four, but almost five," I replied.

"Two Barbie dolls coming up! I will do my best to get those elves on that right away!" Santa said, handing me a candy cane and three more for my siblings.

"Merry Christmas, Santa!" I said as I walked confidently towards my family.

"How did that go Diana?" Dad inquired.

"It was okay," I said, spreading the joy of candy canes to my siblings. "Santa called me a boy and greedy for asking for two Barbies!"

Dad pulled me to his side.

"Dad, do I look like a boy?"

"Yeah!" my brothers chimed in at the same time, giggling. Tears welling, I looked to my dad for reassurance.

"Diana, you know we don't have much. You have to wear hand-me-downs, and sometimes those are your brother's old clothes. Kim does too. But no, you do not look like a boy!"

With that, we all fell back into line and followed Dad back to the station wagon. Everyone continued to poke fun at me for being mistaken for a boy, and I even managed a laugh.

Chapter 4

The Breath you Take

My first attack was when I was four. Kim and I were splashing about in the bathtub, one of our favourite pastimes, plus I always liked hair washing night. We had these cute little kids' shampoos Mom would order from the local Avon lady, Bonnie. The bottles had pictures of fawns on them, and the shampoo smelled wonderful! Visits from Mom's Avon lady were always fun as Kim's best friend would tag along. We would play while our moms visited and Mom pondered her order. There were very few things Mom was able to splurge on without Dad cancelling her order, but Avon was one of them.

Kim and I were giggling at the bubbles we had made in the bath when I suddenly felt a heaviness in my chest. There was an odd sound, a wheezing noise, coming from my airway. I felt like I was choking, yet nothing was stuck! Confused, I shot my sister a look of panic while I grabbed the sides of the tub to steady my dizzying head. Kim shrieked for Dad. Everyone but Mom, who was screaming for someone to help me from her wheelchair, converged with lightning speed on our tiny mint green bathroom upstairs.

My dad quickly scooped me out of the tub and wrapped me in a thin cream-coloured towel.

"She's breathing funny," Kim said through her sobs.

Frantic now, Dad carried my limp and naked body to my bedroom, which is down the narrow staircase and to the right, looking for clothes. As I struggled for breath, he hastily wrapped me in my hand-me-down mustard yellow T-shirt that said "Big Jim" and a pair of dark brown corduroy pants. Each breath caused me to make a strange noise while inhaling as air tried to squeak its way inside my tiny lungs.

Until then, I'd never thought about my breath, how I do it and what to do to do it properly. This feeling was foreign to me, and I started to cry as fear settled in. I didn't understand exactly what dying was, but Dad said, "Dean, call the Dodsland Hospital now—tell them she might die!" Dean raced away as I was rushed to our familiar old brown station wagon. Dad held me on his lap while he drove. The only time he'd ever done that before is when he let us steer on the back roads for fun. This time, though, panic hung heavy in the air.

The rest of the kids were left behind with Dean and Mom while Dad, clutching me close to him, drove as fast as our wagon could go down bumpy Highway 31 towards the closest hospital, which was seven miles away. When you can't breathe, seven miles feels like a hundred! When we got there the nurses quickly rushed me into emergency and put something over my face to help me breathe. I was exhausted and wanted to lay down, but the nurses and doctor wouldn't let me. I was given oxygen and two needles.

Once I was stable, Dad came into the little room and sat with me while the doctor explained to us what happened.

"I'm afraid your daughter had an asthma attack," the doctor said rather matter-of-factly. "I will do an X-ray to confirm her lungs are okay, but I expect the diagnosis to be the same. I gave her some medicine in her nebulizer, and it opened her bronchioles right up."

I didn't really listen closely as they discussed my breathing problems because I was exhausted and needed some sleep. Relieved I could breathe again, I let sleep take me into its peaceful arms right on the cold metal hospital bed that was covered with a sheer white sheet. I was clearly drained, so they decided to keep me overnight in the hospital for observation.

Of course, as a newly-diagnosed little four-year-old, I was unable to recall the name of the disease that took my breath away, but I did know that I had no idea what was happening when an attack came on, which frightened me. With layers of disease riddling our family, I was instantly put in charge of my own medication and expected to know the dosage and when to inhale the lifesaving powder to keep the airway goblins at bay. There was no time for me to be sick, of that I was aware.

Shockingly (but not), I almost never remembered where I left my inhalers or how much to take when I found them, so constant scolding ensued. I was a four-year-old left in charge of my life, but I didn't have the capacity to understand what was happening to me nor the skill set required to fulfill a medicine routine. I had two inhalers—one was used if I couldn't breathe and one was to prevent the attacks from coming—and I could never remember which was for which. The attacks scared my family, most of all my dad, and his reaction elevated quickly to anger. It was at these times, during these reactions, where terror bred inside my impressionable mind. Consequently, this is also when I became skilled at trying to manage the attacks on my own.

Upon further investigation into my asthma, it was discovered that I had developed allergies to cats, running was a major trigger, and the dusty grain-filled air of harvest didn't help either. I was pretty much allergic to the outdoors, but that wouldn't stop me. I was a farm kid who ran around outside from sunup to sundown. I played with all our cats and bunnies, of which there were many, and always rode around in the tractor or grain truck with Dad and my siblings. None of this changed, although it probably should have. I had never heard of allergy medications, and the only over-the-counter drugs that were in our house were aspirin, Buckley's Mixture, and Malox (or chalk, as we called it). I was too young to understand what an allergy was, and no one took the time to explain it to me either. This meant there was nothing for me to take to prevent the allergies from grabbing hold of my body at any time.

Several months after my first asthma attack, I caught pneumonia. I was admitted to the hospital again, this time spending ten days in an oxygen tent. I slept a lot and carried a fever through moments of fitful rest. I cried a lot. I'm not sure if it was from the pain, the loneliness, the fear or the fact that I was in a crib. All of these things created distress in my normal smiley and happy demeanour. My nickname as a little girl was "Smiley." I was known for my happiness, but at four years old, that was the last thing I felt.

I was angry I was in a crib. *Only babies use cribs, and I'm no baby, even though my brothers call me one!* Four years old was far too old to be in a crib. I had to endure tubes up my nose and needles every few hours. As much as I received praise for not crying when the needles came, they still hurt and I wanted to cry, but I thought if I didn't cry, maybe my family would come take me home. *Maybe, just maybe, I was a good girl after all.*

What the nurses and doctors didn't understand was that my silence was filled with a deep yearning to cry out in pain, both physical and mental. However, I had been taught to push it down into a deep dark place where no one could see it. This was not in my nature, so I had a royal fit because I was in the crib! I would thrash and cry (wail, in fact) until I drew someone's attention. I blamed the crib for my inexcusable behaviour, but the loneliness was the real root of my nightly howling. Still, I would not tell them of my sadness, they only heard my cries.

The staff at the Dodsland Hospital showed me immense patience, loving tenderness and compassion. My fitful nights did not go on for long as a nurse was soon at my side. Being upset made breathing particularly challenging, so the nurse would come into my room, put her hands through to the armholes of the tent and rub my back while softly offering compassion. Some nurses would unzip the tent, unhook the oxygen, pick me up in their arms, carry me to the rocking chair and rock me tenderly until I fell asleep. Even the chef took a special shining to me, coming into my room to ask me which kind of soup I wanted for lunch. I was on a liquid diet, so there were not many options, but he always made me feel like I was at some sort of fancy restaurant ordering up a dish he would prepare especially for me! It was these small acts of kindness that made me want to help everyone else feel as they made me feel: loved.

It was evident my family would continue on without me, of this I was painfully aware. The nights were long with no one there to sleep with. Kim and I shared a bed at home, so I desperately wanted her there with me to cuddle up to her arm after she fell asleep. (She wasn't a cuddler, so I had to be slow and sneaky with my ways.) I wanted comfort, which the staff was good at during the day, but I struggled with the lonely nights. I felt forgettable and not worth my family's time, which made me feel worthless. At that tender age of four, our minds are not capable of understanding the rational reasons—it's hard to travel with Mom; my siblings have schoolwork; maybe they were running off to hockey or Dad had a curling game—that may have kept them away. I felt I had done something wrong for them not to come, but I didn't know what.

I spent hours waiting to see them. When I wasn't thinking of this reunion, I played with toys once I was allowed out of the oxygen tent, and I stared at the beautiful artwork the Bevans, two talented local artists, did of Snow White and the seven dwarfs on the wall. Sometimes the nurses or the chef would read to me while I nuzzled up tightly to their chest in the rocker in the corner of my room and felt I had no cares in the world. The nights would come again, though, and the great sadness would overtake my small yet tender heart.

I felt everyone else's happiness was more important than mine. All I wanted was my family to visit so I could sit on Dad's lap and, mostly, to not be forgotten. I wanted to be worth remembering, worth visiting, worth loving. The tears came each and every night until one night they didn't.

One night, a nurse led Dad, Mom, Aaron, Chris and Kim to my room! It was a miracle! I was in the oxygen tent, but the nurse quickly unhooked me so I could spend some time with them. Everyone thought my setup was neat, including the oxygen I was getting through the nose. I showed them all the cool toys I could play with, and we all admired the artwork on the walls. I crawled up on Dad's lap, he smiled at me, I hugged him tight. I did not want this night to end. I don't know how long they were there, but they lifted my spirits enough to help me recover.

Dad would always panic when I had an asthma attack. I know now that his reaction was likely from fear, but his fear frightened me at the time. On one hand, I was fearful of asthma stealing my air, and on the other I was even more fearful of my father's temper and the lashing I would get for having an asthma attack and needing his help. I only considered asking for help in my absolutely most desperate situations because I was deeply ashamed to cause more stress for my dad.

When my chest would tighten, my rescue inhaler often wouldn't work. Other times, I emptied the rescue inhaler but found no relief. Taking too much of it resulted in a shaky body caused by too much cortisol in my system. I hated that feeling, but by the time I realized I'd taken too much, there wasn't anything I could do to calm myself down. This compounded my problem. Managing my own medications was not a very good idea, but it was one less stress on Dad's mind.

Laboured breathing accompanied by petrifying fear kept me bound to my bedroom and unable to reach out for help. I never knew how harsh my father's wrath would be if or when I would reach my breaking point and know I could no longer handle the torture of slowly dying. If he was drunk, I may not be able to wake him, and if I did, he would be raging mad. Sober dad meant he was likely hungover or stressed or both, so meeting him in this state was equally fearful. Sadly, this was the battle I fought. While my mind was busy trying to regain control over my body, it was also wrestling with the demons of fear. Regardless of my determination not to tell Dad, I would usually lose this battle because I intuitively knew that if I didn't get to a hospital soon I would not survive. I faced debilitating fear of life or death alone, and this, strangely, became my norm. Asthma became my own dirty little secret; a place I where I battled myself. *Am I worth saving?* I didn't question why the asthma awoke such an angry beast inside my father, but I knew I didn't want to see it and didn't want my siblings to be afraid. I knew I was the cause of it, so I desperately tried to suffer alone in silence and shame.

At fourteen years old, Kim and I were at home by ourselves. Dad was gone for the weekend, Chris no longer lived at home and Aaron was out with friends. Kim and I had spent the day taking turns talking on the phone to various friends to pass our day. It had been warm that day, so the front door that led to the deck was open as none of our windows could open.

I suddenly felt the familiar tightness creep into my chest and lock up my lungs. I laboured through as always, sure I could get myself past it, but something felt different. My rescue inhaler was not helping, and my breathing became sparse and I grew almost too tired to be fearful. I hunched over a pillow, my go-to position, to try to sleep but couldn't. Kim was not allowed to go for her driver's test even though she was sixteen, so we knew she could not get me to the hospital. The idea that I may not be able to get there created an unsettling feeling between us; we had no power, no control. I squeezed my pillow tight as Kim paced the living room floor searching for what to do. When I caught her eyes, I saw that familiar fear. *What are we going to do?* The deep knowing of my soul, which I was first introduced to as a four-year-old through my mother's illness, whispered here again, but this time it warned me that I would not make it without help.

It had been almost two hours, and I did not have much more fight left in me. Looking at Kim, I slowly mouthed out instructions.

"Phone ... our friend," I paused, gasping for more air, "Jodi."

I was barely audible; the sound of wheezing was louder than my words. Kim's eyes widened as if hearing the whispers of my soul. *Death is knocking.* My broken words and half open eyes were desperate. Kim drew closer to catch my final whispers.

"Her parents ... " I said, reaching for any little bit of air I could muster, "... will take me in."

Those words probably saved my life. I didn't allow myself to contemplate why Kimberley hadn't called someone to help already. I accepted that she was a person who needed direction. She did as I requested, and Jodi's mom arrived at the farm about ten minutes later. It's only a five-minute drive, but she got lost on her way there. A sense of relief wafted into my frail body as Kim said, "She's here," her voice excited for us both. Small sips of air had kept me alive for almost three hours, and I was lightheaded and exhausted, but the whisper was back. *Almost there, Diana. Keep steady; help is here.*

I knew it was bad from the look on Jane's face when she walked in and saw me.

"Oh my God, Diana!"

Clearly, she had never seen me in this state before.

"Where is your Dad? Did anyone call him? Kim, I need you to come with me. Can you help me carry her to the car?"

Jane's words were thick with fear, and I instinctually knew she was thinking, *Am I too late?*

Don't worry Jane, I thought, *I've been thinking the same thing.* But I can't get my thoughts to words. Strangely enough, this moment leads me to make a connection I hadn't before: *Is this how Mom feels?*

Clumsily, they each take hold of either side of my body, working together to lift me to the vehicle. The humid and heavy summer air hits me hard, and I lunge forward attempting to regain what little air I had been able to handle in the house. I contemplate if it's better to fight through the feeling of suffocating to live or just give in to the freedom of death. The battle between my mind and heart was very real. *If I made my mother sick, I may well deserve this torturous death.* Tears stain my cheeks; no one else will know the heaviness inside my lungs is a result of guilt.

As we arrived at the hospital, my mind allowed me to entertain hope knowing I would receive the lifesaving medication I desperately needed. You can imagine how devastated I was to find out I was wrong. The nurses were used to seeing me in the emergency room—this was a familiar routine—but as my weary eyes looked into theirs, I saw the same fear I saw in Jane's eyes. Most times, there was a quiet reassurance which calms me. This time, however, is far worse, even though there had been plenty of close calls.

When worthlessness pitched its tent in my psyche, it didn't just camp out for a day or two; it embedded itself in my soul. Eventually, it built it's home. It seeped into every inch of my mind, filling my head with unloving self-talk. This one action of neglect spurred on years of self-torture, bad decisions and self-sabotage. When someone good came into my life to love me, I could not understand why they would ever want to stay. I wasn't worth saving, so why would anyone want to waste their time?

No one ever said, "You aren't worth saving," but the words were in their actions and in my own. I felt more like an imposition and burden—there was no time to save a little girl who was suffering in her own personal suffocation chamber. Such is the young mind. Worth in our household was a battlefield not something entitled to you for being alive. No, quite the opposite. It was a spot you had to earn, but it was ever illusive, a moving target, a dark shadow in the depths of your soul and the cancer of our family.

When I look at self-worth—when I look at my self-value and where it comes from—I have to look deep inside. I feel I am the product of each situation, each circumstance, where people who held some sort of authority or position higher in society than me judged me. Falsely, I believed my value came from other people's beliefs of who I was and who I was to become. I collected each and every stone cast in judgement and placed them in the pockets of my soul. Every year, or week, or day, or hour, or minute—each second!—people handed those stones to me for free, and I somehow felt it was my duty to carry the weight of this judgmental world. A duty laced with shame and guilt. The stones were heavy. They weighed me down. But what happens when you carry something heavy? Do you become stronger? Maybe you feel you have no choice. One thing I know for sure, you do become tired.

My parents wove my self-worth into my being at a very young age. Neglect, violence, abuse and addiction all played a vital role in how I saw myself. As a child, I tended to be more selfish, and I took situations into my mind, my heart, like their beliefs were my own. There was no other compass of reference than what my family did, said and believed. That is the influence of family.

I blamed myself. I believed I was bad and that I deserved the chaos that was enveloping me. This was due to my lack of understanding and trying to justify why some things happened. It was an attempt to find answers. I took paths without thinking, frantically searching for a place to belong. Lonely and misunderstood, I sought shelter from my storm in those who professed love but did not love me.

When this pattern of people pleasing and accepting crumbs of love started in my childhood, I thought it was normal. It was so second nature that I had no idea I was doing it. I only knew I was frustrated by getting the same results and was locked in a conditioned pattern of doubting myself and my abilities. This was self-sabotage at its finest, and I was guilty of it for many years. Others may have thought I was self-absorbed, but people like me internalize situations that we have no control over and blame ourselves. Until I dealt with my past trauma and pain, I continued to cycle through this storyline over and over again, playing it out with new characters but familiar situations.

The nurse nervously averted her eyes from my panicked stare and carried me, with some help, to the generic, whitewashed walls of the emergency room. Pale pink curtains that hung like they were waiting for me gave the illusion of privacy. I knew this room like the back of my hands. To the right was the cupboard with the nebulizer paraphernalia, sterile and wrapped in plastic. Locked in a starch white cabinet secured to the wall lay the vile of life-saving medication I urgently needed. Just being in this room gave me a bit of hope that relief was in reach. Beside my bed was the oxygen the nurse was hooking me up to. My life hung in the balance of the valued contents within that small, cool room. It was ready for me. There was a limited window of opportunity to get medicine into my body in order to open up my lungs—we all knew that—but time seemed to be against me.

I had waited too long to ask for help, so my body weaker than usual. One of the nurses rushed into the room and urgently whispered into the head nurse's ear. The news didn't seem good because they both turned to Jane and motioned for her to follow them into the hallway. Kim sat on a stool in the corner of the room looking at me and then the door. They had never left the room to discuss me before. Panic once again jumped out of my mind and into my already tight lungs while fearful tears fell to the fluffy cotton pillow. I knew what this meant and, defeated, I was ready to give up. Death looked like the easier option. Kim saw this and quickly walked to the door. She leaned in close and repeated what she heard to me.

"We have a problem. There is no doctor in this weekend—he is away at a convention. We've tried to reach him, but no one is answering," Kim repeated from the whispers in the hallway. "Without doctor authorization we cannot legally give the medication to Diana. We know, though, without the medication, she will not survive."

As Kim finished the whispered words to me, we both looked at each other with a sickening stare. Kim's eyes met mine and welled with tears. She quickly wiped her cheeks with the back of her thin hands and sat back down on the stool as the group re-entered the room.

The nurse approached, careful not to alarm me. She rubbed my back with her soft hands in an attempt to relieve the tightness that's enwrapped my chest. With the gentleness of a true nurse, she allowed her humanness to reach out to mine. Her other hand reached for my chin and guided my turned-down face full of tears and hopelessness towards her soft and loving eyes. Guided by her heart, she let the words hit the air. "Sweetheart, we don't have a doctor here. He is gone this weekend." I was trapped in a tug of war. My body was forcing me to die, to cave, to allow the disease to wrap its suffocating grip around my neck and choke me to death while my soul was willing me to fight, to push past the odds, to choose to live. Moving her hands to rub my tired and tear-stained cheeks, she continued, "But it's okay, Sweetie, we got you."

I wasn't sure either of us believed that.

The fear of death hung heavy in the room. I wondered where it was coming from before I realized it was me. It was getting hard to see, figures became fuzzy and my legs felt different, numb. I was light-headed and hunched over my pillow. Exhaustion settled in as my breathing became shallower than I ever remember. I felt tired and wanted to sleep; I knew I could, which was also a strange feeling. This was a new experience, one I struggle to put words to. It was fear mixed with a quiet acceptance that I may in fact die there. No parents to hold my hand. Dad didn't even know what was happening. We had no way to reach him, no phone number to call. We were alone in this, just Kimberley and me. Much of our lives had been spent like this, yet I yearned for my father to know, to care, to deem me worth saving.

Jodi's mom looked at me then the nurse as I slowly lifted my head. It took all my effort to raise my face to them, silent tears streaming down my puffy cheeks to my blue lips. The monitors showed gravely low oxygen levels. Everyone knew I was closer to death than to life, so the decision was clear: administer the medication without doctor approval.

The nurses worked quickly, almost in a frightful state, as they saw how close I was to falling over and laid me back on the upright bed. The weakness took over as the lids of my eyes slid closed. I could hear the commotion as the nurse fiddled with her keys to unlock the cabinet that held the medicine; everything was loud and quiet at the same time. It was strange. I was dancing with death.

One nurse prepped my arm to administer drugs straight to my bloodstream while the other opened the medication then adjusted my nebulizer so I would breathe in the other medication. Slowly, my shackled airways welcomed both the medication and oxygen. I was relieved, exhausted and more frightened than I had ever been. Never had I been that close to death. It could have gone either way. Sure enough, shortly after I started breathing, the doctor called the hospital back. The nurse explained what she did and, of course, the doctor knew she had no other choice. I would not have survived had she waited.

Thinking back now, I understand that asthma embedded a determination and resiliency into my heart. When you can't breathe, you can't just ignore it. Asthma demands your immediate attention. It's unrelenting and unforgiving. It forces you to dance at the doorstep of death at a moment's notice. I learned this very quickly as each time I would be rushed to emergency, I would be whisked away, ahead of everyone else that was waiting. Fear was the emotion that met everyone in my presence. They knew if the asthma was left untreated it would show no mercy and most likely kill me.

Each attack asked me an important question: Are you worth saving? My answer was "No," which was why I usually waited too long to ask for help. I was also deathly afraid of my father. I hated asking for help, so I allowed fear to take over my rational mind and embed the notion that I am worthless in my soul. It haunts me to this day.

My father put all the responsibility of my disease management and care squarely on my shoulders from the moment I was diagnosed. When I was too little to even remember the name of the illness, I was expected to master self-medication and breathing. To say that I didn't have the capacity to handle it is laughable—I was four years old! I quickly learned to associate shame with asking for help because it meant I was not doing what was asked of me, that I could not take care of myself, and that I became a burden instead of "useful." I desperately wanted to be thought of as useful. I wanted to help my father with all his stress, not add to it. Therefore, asthma was a weakness. At the first sign of a tight chest, I would hide in my messy bedroom and rifle through each and every corner in hopes of finding my little blue inhaler. Most of the time, I turned up empty handed or with an empty inhaler. In any case, I had to keep this to myself and vow not to upset my father, not show my weakness, and to handle this attack like I handled the other areas of my life: alone or with only my siblings.

Fear short-circuited my logic and clear thinking. I associated my father's reactions with worth. A positive reaction meant I was useful, serving a purpose to the family. Sadly, I was met with his rage reaction much of the time, which I then internalized. This is the root of my people pleasing. This is why I cared more about what others thought of me than what I thought of myself. This is where I lost myself.

Chapter 5

I Care

Dad was no stranger when it came to advertising in *The Western Producer*. Hiring someone to care for our mom and then us children after she went into a home was no easy task in the '80s. My mom needed extensive care before going into permanent care. Her needs were a full time job. When Dad hired a caregiver, we understood they were there for Mom, not to meet our needs. That being said, almost everyone Dad brought into our home always did double duty. They would see us kids and immediately roll into mothering. I cannot speak for them, but I sense this was natural.

Our needs were always looked after when the caregivers could fit us in. It may not have been by giving us their time or attention, although some did. No, sometimes it came in the form of discipline and standards. We weren't the tidiest kids, and our rooms were often piled up with clothes, toys and other miscellaneous items. Dean was always firm about us cleaning our rooms and helping with chores. There were days I would try to avoid her by going outside to play far away from the tall white farmhouse—usually down by the mountain ash trees near the dugout filled with murky water—before she would arrive at 9:00 a.m. The dugout housed things like the old thrasher combine, which amused us kids for hours, keeping our imagination sharp with boundless games. We didn't keep close tabs on time, and hours could pass while we were in the throes of imagination before we paid any attention to the pangs of hunger. When the cowbell rang, we knew chores were to be done or it was lunch or supper time. That old cow bell still hangs on our old farmhouse many years later waiting for the next generation to ring the call of supper.

Dean was with our family the longest by far. She was with us when Mom was living at home and then off and on after that. She made the best buns and chocolate chip cookies, and she made us supper every night before she went home.

Dean was strict. She had rules, and we kept our opinions about those rules to ourselves. Respect was important to her, and we did as we were told—or so I remember. She would reward us with ice cream pails full of cookies, saskatoon berry pies and fresh picked produce. Even though she liked things her way and we had to do what felt like a ton of work to get it just so, we secretly liked the discipline. It gave me a good feeling to have a clean bedroom to sleep in and fresh baking to eat. I mostly liked feeling like we were like everyone else—like we had a normal household; that's all I wanted. Dean gave us that sense of security and normalcy that we craved without even understanding it. She allowed us our childhood freedom once our chores were done, and we could build forts, play hide-and-seek outside or enjoy running around with the animals. We could do whatever our imagination could think of while Dean worked away at making sure everyone's clothes were mended and the household needs were met. She ran a tight ship, but there was security in that tightness. To this day, I am deeply grateful to her for making our childhood more normal.

Not all ads proved fruitful. In fact, some hires were utterly dreadful! One woman and her son came by bus from Ontario to live with us. Well, not live in the house but in our small camper on the farm, on a trial basis. That's a long way to travel for a "trial basis." I secretly wondered if Dad may have thought this woman would start out as our caregiver and easily transition into something more. After all, that is how Dad's parents met. Grandpa hired Grandma as his cleaner! Dad was also a sucker for a person with a sad story, and although I never asked what ghosts from her past haunted her, Dad said life had not been kind to her. She was looking to start a new life, and this was her clean slate.

Unfortunately, everything about Sunday (yes, you read that right) being in our home felt uneasy. I learned to read energy and trust my intuition at a young age, and hers was heavy; it didn't mesh with our family. I felt uncomfortable and also quickly figured out that she did not like me. I could not put my finger on exactly what was wrong or why we didn't seem to get along, but the unease within my small body would not dissipate. It spoke to me this way: *She is not here to stay. She is not who she says she is.*

Her son was dark: he dressed all in black and wore one black leather glove with the fingers cut off on his left hand. As curious as I was, I never asked why he would wear just one glove, especially in August when the heat hung heavily in the air like smog in the city skies. And why wear just one? This unusual choice of clothing was foreign to me and proved interesting to my siblings and me as we often conjured up theories as to what the single gloved hand meant. The boys were sure it was a fad linked to Michael Jackson. According to the show *Video Hits*, where Michael Jackson videos were on regular rotation, this was plausible. I suppose we could have asked the one-gloved gothic teenager why, but that would be too direct, something none of us were comfortable with.

Instead of staying at home during that week of summer holidays, I disliked her so much I spent most of that week hauling grain to the local Wheat Pool grain elevator with my dad. The elevator agent, Walter, was such a kind and attentive man, so I knew jumping in the grain truck with Dad meant I got to visit with him. I liked watching as he weighed the load and filled out the paperwork all the while chit-chatting with me about how my day was going. It didn't matter if we were at the elevator five times that day, he always made time to make me feel important.

Unlike Dean, Sunday didn't enjoy baking, cooking or cleaning, issues Dad immediately noticed. Kind of hard not to when you come in from a long day's work in the field and supper is not made; this was supposed to be her job. I made no qualms about sharing my feelings about Sunday with our dad. I could always talk with him, and that week spent together in the grain truck offered plenty of time to share my displeasure. She lasted less than a week and back on the bus she went! I'm not sure where she ended up, but I knew she was gone and we were all happier for it. The house could breathe again. I suppose that was the risk of hiring someone you've never actually met; you never know what you're going to get until you pick them up from the Greyhound bus!

There were times, however, when the newspaper proved its worth. One of my favourite caregivers, Darla, responded to my father's ad. A beautiful young woman in her early twenties, Darla lived a half hour away in a community called Kerrobert. She was a university student and ended up spending summer with us. Kim and I were confused about what "girly" activities were, but we quickly learned. Darla was handy with a sewing machine, and she set up my mother's Singer she had gotten for her wedding. Coincidentally, my name was stenciled on the side: DIANA. I thought I was named after the captivating Princess of Wales, and Aaron said I was named after the famous singer Brenda Lee (middle name), but somehow I've always known I was named after a clunky old sewing machine I could never bond with to make anything that even closely resembled clothing. However, Darla made that Singer sing, pardon the pun. Guiding the small material past the needle, she made Kim and I the most stunning Barbie dresses! As simple as the small, pink A-line dresses were, they were simply wonderful to us. I always wanted different clothes than what came with Barbie, and Darla made that dream happen. Her presence was a joy as she lifted morale in the house during that long, hot summer. I know we all secretly wished our time together would never end, but she went back to university that fall and never returned.

Ruby was another caregiver, although I don't think she replied to the ad in the paper because she lived close by. Ruby loved to laugh and hug, and she was never short on words. Our hearts were captivated with her joyous presence and riveting stories. Kim and I particularly enjoyed the days she brought a small sample of her nail polish collection. As she painted our nails, she told us of all the nail colours she had in her home—it sounded like a wonderland to my sister and me. We really enjoyed her company. She could even make our serious older brother Aaron laugh, and I know both my brothers enjoyed her attentive hugs. She had a way of making a kid feel special, wanted and not at all like the burden we surely thought we were.

Chapter 6

Sunday Nights

Winter evenings on the cold, barren prairie could be long for a child. Too cold and dark to go outside, but nothing to do inside. Well, I shouldn't say nothing, but we were expected to use our imaginations and creativity otherwise Dad would put us to work, which was the last thing I wanted to do. Of course, there was supper to be made; it did not matter if you were only eight years old, a three-course meal was an expectation, not a choice, and there was simply no one else to do it. My signature dish was Shake 'n Bake chicken drumsticks, mashed potatoes and canned creamed corn. Kim always dressed her mashed potatoes in the creamed corn, much to my disgust. Ironically, she hated her foods touching. Teasing often ensued when it came to Kim's very routine and systematic regiment of eating.

Once in a while Dad would come home from Plenty with some Kingo Bingo cards which he had purchased at the local Lucky Dollar grocery store. You're probably wondering what this is. Well, instead of loading up in a vehicle to head to a local bingo hall, you purchased bingo cards at the grocery store, tuned into CFQC TV at 6:00 p.m., laid your cards out, grabbed your bingo dabber (or pennies, which is what we used), and played bingo on TV! We would sometimes have TV dinners, which was a welcomed break from making meals. Dad would bring home a stack of cards and several suppers for us to heat up in the oven. I looked forward to the dessert, which was usually a version of Black Forest cake without the icing. Warm and gooey, the cake melted in my mouth at first forkful. We would set up our TV trays in the living room so we could eat and play.

Greg Barnsley was the bingo caller most Saturday nights. He was also the local weatherman from CFQC (or was it QC8 back then?). Listening to the weather report on the radio or TV was the most important part of the day because Dad's income depended on those reports and how they aligned with the skies. Greg was a natural bingo caller, making small talk with the audience and ensuring we all knew the latest weather.

"Under the 'B' ... '8'!"

Down in the lower right corner, you could see the tips of his fingers and the bingo ball, marked with the number he just called. Ever happy and always bright, Greg Barnsley called the numbers until someone called in a bingo on the telephone. We would all wait with bated breath, hoping the bingo was no good, as we usually only had a number or two ourselves left to cover up. We never won Kingo Bingo, but it sure was fun trying, and it broke up our long winters' night.

On the evenings when Dad wasn't in his shop or at the bar, we would all converge in the living room, waiting to see what was on the two channels we got on our television. The best TV of the entire weekend was on Sunday evenings. Unlike today, where there are channels dedicated to cartoons 24/7, we only saw cartoons Saturday mornings and maybe Sunday evenings. We would tune in as a family to watch *The Wonderful World of Disney*, which could range from *The Swiss Family Robinson* to *Lady and the Tramp*.

As you've seen, chaos tended to ride shotgun in our family station wagon most days, but we still managed to have our moments of routine. These were the moments we looked forward to as a family, times where we could be like every everyone else. We popped some popcorn and sat around the TV watching *Dallas*, *Dynasty* or evening cartoons; maybe we even laughed a little. These moments sit in time and are some of my fondest memories. Sometimes you truly don't know the significance of a moment until it becomes a memory.

Chapter 7

Scream

The yellow Ford van glided over the broken pavement with our whole family tucked inside, but this wasn't our usual trip to Dodsland. First off, Dad usually took us to Plenty or Kindersley as that was where he did all his business such as grocery shopping and banking. We didn't usually go to Dodsland unless we were visiting the hospital because of an asthma attack or something to do with Mom's family. She grew up on a farm several miles south of Dodsland and took her schooling there. It is not far from our farm, only seven miles to the west.

I was seven years old, and I sensed something was off. Dad was quiet, as we all were. We pulled up in front of the Dodsland Union Hospital, but I wasn't having an asthma attack. This confused me. We all got out of the car, and Dad pulled out Mom's wheelchair. That's when I noticed the suitcases tucked behind. The boys didn't seem shocked by them and each grabbed one.

"Don't take those out yet, Mom doesn't know!" Dad said harshly.

Dad opened the passenger side door and unbuckled Mom from her seat, saying nothing. My young mind was trying to put together what was happening, but the boys' faces are solemn, they can't make eye contact; it was like their eyes were glued to the sidewalk. Even though my mind was young, my senses were sharp, something honed through having to figure out what Mom needed without her using words or even sign language.

We were greeted by smiling nurses, most of whom I knew as I'd stayed there many times because of my asthma. They were so kind and caring, but my young senses once again picked up something strange behind their smiles. As Aaron pushed mom inside, I was surprised to see Auntie Bernice, Dad's sister. This really didn't make sense. The nurses took us kids to a room about three doors down the hall on the left side; room 6. It's not an examining room, but a room for patients. I'd only ever stayed in the children's room, and I loved it there with the walls full of Disney characters, the books and toys, and a small tub that was just my size. This room looked nothing like that. I didn't know why we'd been brought in there, and I started to wonder where our parents were. Auntie Bernice followed us, which still made zero sense!

Everyone tried to engage in small talk, including the nurses. All of us were clearly nervous, and the boys still hadn't looked up from the floor. Aunty directed them to get the bags from the van, and they briefly leave.

I figured my parents were at an appointment for Mom with the doctor until I saw the boys walk back in with all the bags. I'd stayed in the hospital before and usually didn't have anything other than a hospital gown to stay in. *Whose clothes are in those bags?* I wonder. I looked around, and Auntie Bernice was gone too; it was just us kids. The hospital was silent, but we suddenly heard a blood-curdling scream—a scream we knew. It was our mother; something was wrong! Panic met my adrenaline as I shot up off the bed and raced to the door. The boys stopped me, telling us Mom and Dad would be in there soon and we would know what's going on. The screams didn't stop—they played over and over like a broken record. I heard barely audible moans of "No" mixed with wailing, defiant cries. My nervous energy amplified to sheer panic and questions rolled out fast and furious as the boys tried to calm me and ensure I didn't cause myself an asthma attack. Kim, on the other hand, sat docile on a chair. *Why isn't she freaking out?*

The nurses could hear the commotion in the other room and our mother's panic, from their nurses station, so they came back to check on us kids. They tried to talk about things like school and sports, but all I could do was watch the door. After what seems like an eternity, Mom appeared in the doorway, Dad pushing her in her wheelchair and Auntie Bernice behind them both. Their tear-streaked faces told my young mind that things were about to get worse.

"This is Mom's new home now," Dad said very quietly. "She has to stay here."

As quiet as he said this, the words erupted like thunder in my heart. Kim sank deeper into the shadows of her chair, still emotionless. I was all over the room, unable to contain myself, yet no words escaped me. I looked at my brothers and knew they already knew, their eyes still settled on the floor. Mom was crying, but there are no more wailing tears. All I wanted to do was crawl up on her lap and never let go, but I didn't. I knew better than to show my feelings with words, but my mind appeared to have its own agenda, darting me around the room until Aaron raised his eyes. The exchange settled me, and I stopped dead in my tracks. My intuition was back, bringing with it the knowledge that no matter what I said, I needed to accept this situation. I swallowed the enormous lump in my throat, nestled in beside my sister's corner of reclusion and joined my brothers, staring blankly at the floor.

Several strained minutes later, once Mom's clothes were unpacked into the dresser and closet, Dad said it was time to go home. Going home this time meant without our mom, and the pain surfaces again as tears brimmed in my eyes. I quickly wiped them away with the back of my hand. We all gave mom a hug and left her behind in her room with a couple of nurses. The wailing cries started again, louder and more pained. This was torture for us all, but we marched forward. Nothing can be done.

The ride home was silent, filled with a kind of silent pain that words cannot describe to this day. When we got home, I ran up to my room, opened my window and sat on the ledge that is barely wide enough to hold my tiny bottom in place. As my feet dangled freely, I silently wished the small maple growing below was big enough to bear my weight, close enough to rest by mind and sit awhile. Finally, I did what I had longed to do all day, I cried. So many tears. I'd never been good at hiding, but for some reason this family wanted me to swallow my world of hurt, confusion and pain. I knew then this was not my nature. I could not repress. If I did, I felt uneasy. It felt like I didn't belong in my skin. I realized that what I needed and what my dad needed from me were completely different. Being the child meant I was unable to voice my pain because there was no room for emotions in a household full of booze, financial hardships and sickness, so I learned to supress.

Dad didn't come inside the house, choosing instead to work on something in the shop to divert his attention from the woman he had loved for so long. The shop wasn't a good enough distraction, though, and as I looked out the window, I saw him drive away; there was no question as to where he was going.

The bar became a nightly occurrence most weeks because Dad struggled to handle all the financial, health and poor crops stress. Life just never seemed to look up. Mom had become sick with a nameless illness, but when she got sick, two people got sick. Dad's illness was alcoholism.

Chapter 8

The Knock

The day the knock came I had no idea what was happening. The woman standing at the door looked so striking, and I liked her shoes and clothes. "She looked 'classy,'" my dad said to me later. There was a distinct shift in the energy in the days leading up to the knock. I sensed panic mixed with fear. When you grow up with a non-verbal parent, you tend to sense feelings rather than relying on words. Everyone had to make sure their bedrooms were clean—and I mean nothing-under-your-bed clean! This had us working for two days straight before the visitor arrived. None of us were very impressed with all the work, but I was secretly pleased with how my bedroom looked when it was clean.

My head met my dad's midsection as I stood close, eyeing up the woman as he opened the door. Dad slipped sideways, welcoming her into our home. I shuffled over unnoticed by Dad, but the woman poked her head around to see me standing there. I smiled with my proud seven-year-old grin with a space between my two big frong teeth as I said hello. Her face softened and I felt my eyes brighten. I saw the look between this lady and my dad and sensed this was serious, but I just wanted to be happy, as is my nature. Life between these four walls didn't scream happy much. I didn't understand the word "stress," but it seemed to be commonly said these days. Maybe that's what I sensed.

Dad guided her to the dining room, which actually flowed right into the living room. The boys were already situated on the couch as Dad hollered for Kim. She was upstairs in her room, probably doing art. The coffee, white powdery stuff and sugar were sitting neatly on the long brown 70s style table. Dad usually had his three cups of coffee in the morning and that was it for the day, so this was odd. Also, the table was only set like that when my mom's parents came over to play crib. There was certainly nothing usual about that day.

I sat down in my spot—everyone at the table had "their" spot. The lady asked lots of questions, but they were easy to answer.

"What grade are you in?"

"How do you like school?"

"What do you like to do for fun?"

All the while she was marking things down on paper, but I couldn't read it from where I was sitting. Later, the boys told me she was writing down our answers to her questions, but I was still baffled.

She took Kimberley and me into the back corner of the living room where the encyclopedias and dust merrily gathered, peacefully going unnoticed and undisturbed. It was a corner my brothers went to once in a while if they'd been assigned a homework project that required research. The sconce lit up the panel board wall as our dad, at the woman's request, set up a TV tray. She then kindly placed colourful crayons and glistening white paper on top of it, much to our delight! I knew I liked this lady!

She asked us to draw a picture of our family, and I created stick figures for each one of us, not particularly caring that the heads were disproportionate to the bodies. I drew myself first: short, big head, big hazel eyes and a dark brown bowl-style haircut. There was always a debate about the colour of my eyes—were they green or hazel? I didn't know the difference. Next, I drew Kim: taller than me, bright blue eyes and sandy blond hair. I was unhappy with my yellow; it wasn't the right shade. As I looked over to see Kim's artwork, I felt instantly jealous and a little more than sheepish and what I had created. Kim's drawing was clearly nicer, so I used my arm to cover my paper in the hopes the nice lady wouldn't see.

I was annoyed; I wanted to know how Kim drew the hardest part of our family picture, Mom's wheelchair. Her lines were soft, the bodies of her people not just a mixture of sticks going every which direction. She even managed to draw lips and noses that looked like lips and noses! Somehow the wheelchair looked normal, and she put Mom sitting in it, looking happy. I, on the other hand, drew two big wheels and some sort of chair; I couldn't sort out how to put Mom's stick person in the chair, which left me agitated.

The lady keeps talking to us, in a calm voice, and she asks a bunch of questions. She wanted to know all sorts of things.

"Where do you like to go together as a family?" she asked.

"We sometimes go to Kindersley—to the A&W," I said. "I loved when we parked under the giant awning, then some cool ladies on roller skates came to our window and took our order! Dad had to unroll the window when all the drinks came so the nice waitresses could set the tray on the edge of our window. Our whole family was shocked when the heavy tray full of frosty glasses filled to the brim with bubbly root beer didn't break the window because of its weight! Next, they came wheeling over with our meals—Kim and I always got the same: a Balloon Pack which has a cheeseburger and fries in a box with a balloon fastened to the top. It is my favourite place to go. I also like going to the mall to get clothes, but we don't go often," I said with a sigh. "Peavey Mart, now that is Dad's favourite store, and every time we go to Kindersley, we stop there. Dad also makes us go through all the tractor dealerships, which I find particularly boring. When we go into the stores, one of us has to stay in the vehicle with Mom because Dad says it is too much work to get her out of the vehicle and he didn't want her alone. Sometimes Dad takes us all in; those days are special. Mom likes going to see all the pretty decorations in the stores at Christmas especially. I don't always like when she comes in with us," I confessed. "Lots of people stare, they look at Mom like they've never seen a sick person before!" I was getting angry. "They think I don't notice, but I do and I don't like it."

The nice lady's lips parted slightly and she let a small sigh out. Her eyes filled with compassion as she reached over to take a look at my picture.

"It's not finished yet," I explained.

"It's hard to draw a wheelchair, isn't it?" the nice lady said.

"It's even harder to push one," I stated truthfully.

Our eyes met again and we were drawn back to the picture, which was simple yet confused—exactly how I felt.

Kim had been quietly drawing the entire time, which was not out of the ordinary. The lady tried to engage her; Kim's remarks were short but honest. She didn't meet the nice lady's eyes, instead focusing only on her artwork. I secretly chastised Kim in my mind for not talking more to this very nice lady. She never talks much to many people. I usually talk for the both of us.

"Kim loves art, so don't take it personally," I said. "Usually, I can't pull her away from her pencil crayons to play Barbies."

The lady gently asked to see Kim's artwork, and Kim bashfully surrendered her piece from her clutches. The lady's eyes widened at what Kim had been busy working on while we chatted.

"This is fantastic, Kimberley! You are very good!"

Kim sheepishly smiled, briefly looking up. I was jealous and proud all at once. It felt mixed up inside me. I wanted the attention, but I also knew the lady was right; Kim's work was great and she deserved the praise, so I put the wolf of jealousy to bed in the peaceful joy of Kim's accomplishment.

Soon we were left in the corner to keep working away at our pictures so the nice lady could speak with our brothers. Their conversation seemed to last forever, and I wondered if they, too, got nice crayons like us. When it was time to say goodbye, I hung close beside my dad as we walked her to the door. Dad thanked her for coming.

"You have a nice family, Leslie. Very nice kids. You are doing the best you can considering the hard circumstances you face," she said.

Dad, looking the most relieved I had seen all day, smiled a genuine grin and breathed a sigh of relief.

"I don't feel there is a need to take these children from their home at this time, Leslie. You are all doing just fine. We will be checking on you, though, because your circumstances are tough and we need to ensure the kids are safe."

I felt my dad may melt in his own skin, his hand clutched mine and gave it a soft squeeze. We didn't dare meet eyes, but I sensed happiness. I knew this was good news.

As the door closed behind the pleasant lady, Dad turned to face me, a smile spread across his tanned skin. He then yelled for the rest of the kids to meet him in the living room. The boys, wringing their hands and looking worried as they walked in, settled uncomfortably on the edge of our taupe sofa with the flower pattern. I saw their fear. Neither of them could meet Dad's weathered green eyes, which tells me they must have known what the lady's visit was about. Dad took his seat on the brown rocking chair, and I crawled up on his lap as I sometimes liked to do. Kim joined me on the other side, Dad rocking us both gently as he rounded his hands across our small frames. Dad cleared his throat and finally spoke.

"That lady was from social services," he said. "Someone put in a complaint about a father raising kids, and they were told to investigate us."

I didn't understand what he meant, and the boys still did not look up.

"She was happy with what she saw here today," he continued. "I told her nothing bad is going on in this house. We haven't had it easy, but we all know what we have to do and just do it. I bet it was that teacher that reported us to them. He's had it out for us for years! She said they had reports that you kids weren't being fed! You go to school with a lunch—a sandwich and an apple—nothing fancy, but it's food!"

His reassured tone was more for him than us. I noticed the other kids had Fruit Roll-Ups, hard cheese and pudding cups. I wanted those in my lunch, too, but I knew not to expect those things.

Dad then explained that if anything happened to him, we would end up in the hands of social services as no one in the family wanted to take four kids; there were just too many of us. Plus, if we ended up in the foster care system, we would be split up. The social worker told Dad that if they decided to take us away, they would try to keep two of us together, but four was impossible. If the movie *Annie* taught me anything, it was that I did not want to go into foster care. I winced at the notion of not having Dad or my siblings. I also now understood why Dad, Aaron and Chris were so anxious all day; this situation was scary. Even though I hadn't been told what was going on, I relied on my senses to gauge the situation, just like I always had. My gut always led me to the right conclusions.

Dad assured us this wasn't going to happen unless he died, but he also left me with an ominous warning.

"If we are not careful, they will take you away. The social worker told me they will be watching us, making sure you guys are safe."

With that, the conversation ended and we dispersed to our bedrooms to be alone with our thoughts.

I laid awake that night plagued with thoughts of losing Dad, so I sneaked into Kim's bedroom, crawled into her bed and cuddled close in hopes of receiving comfort from being next to her, but she pushed me away. So I did what I always did: I waited until she was fast asleep before slowly, carefully slipping her arm around me. I knew I could not live without her, and I held her tight for as long as I could. With Mom gone, I already knew what it was like to have the family split up, and I did not like it. A life without my family was not a life I wanted to live.

Chapter 9

West Edmondon Road Trip

Time seemed to slow down in the summer when I was a child. I enjoyed my days of make-believe, shadow tag and digging in the dirt to make swimming pools for Barbie. I was often lonesome, for what I could not say because I was surrounded by siblings and animals most days. Yet there was still this deep, innate yearning, like I was missing a piece of something I could not explain. Looking back, it's clear I was yearning for Mom.

Dad was aware that Kim and I should have a female influence in our lives. There were a few aunts and even one of his cousins who would take us in for a few weeks during the summer or over Easter break. It gave us all a break from each other and the lengthy, repetitive days of the farm.

By far my favourite place to visit was Mom's sister, Betty. Auntie Betty had three older kids with my uncle Walt. They owned a farm a few miles from the Alberta/Saskatchewan border, on the Alberta side, about 2.5 hours away from our house. The drive up was always beautiful with winding highways pulling us north and lush prairie grasses waving hello in the wind. The sunshine danced against the glass of our van windshield, forming rainbows along the uneven cracks and foreshadowing the bright, fun-filled days that laid ahead.

My favourite thing about spending time at Auntie's house was receiving attention from everyone, but mostly my aunt. Whether it was baking, helping clean up or taking a drive off the farm to Lloydminster for a movie, lunch out or a bit of shopping, I always knew I was important when I walked through her door. Life was busy for them, but I never once felt like I was an imposition or that there was no time for me.

The smell of buns or cookies always met my nose when I raced into their house, dropping my belongings in a heap on their floor in the porch in search of the hug I knew was waiting for me. I was an affectionate child who loved hugs but rarely got them. I'd hop up the two small steps to the main floor and find my auntie and uncle smiling brightly as their three children, Kev, Emma and Jay, sat around the island doing homework.

"Hi there, Sweetie," Uncle Wally would say, nestling me in his arms.

I couldn't help but smile at this embrace. Auntie was next, arms wide and full of love.

"Diana, I think you've grown a little," she'd say, holding me back enough to get a good look at me. "Come to the measuring wall; let's see how much you've grown since last time you were here!"

With that, I would grab the ruler and pencil, which was neatly placed in the drawer of their custom-made oak desk in the kitchen and meet her around the corner.

Their home was always tidy, and I felt a true sense of belonging from the moment we drove into their equally tidy yard. Everyone there had a way of making me feel special, and they made sure we knew we were loved. Once we walked through their door, we were met with a landing to go to the basement or two steps up to the main floor. I loved their living room as it was two steps up from the dining room and provided an excellent stage for Kimberley and me to entertain the family with made up plays or songs.

In the summer of 1988, a plan was forged between my dad and my aunt for us four kids to join her and her family on a trip to West Edmonton Mall for the day! The biggest mall I had ever been to was in Kindersley and it only had three stores we frequented—SAAN,

Zellers and the OK Economy grocery store! I had heard on the news and that West Edmonton Mall was the biggest mall in the world. Apparently, it even had a wave pool (which was cool, but I had never taken swimming lessons) and an amusement park inside—what a foreign concept!

When I could see Edmonton in the distance, I had this genuine feeling of childlike excitement, something I rarely experienced. I distinctly remember wanting to bottle up the way I felt so I could sip it into my heart when things were hard back at home. The excitement bubbled up from deep inside, and I could almost taste it.

My aunt had brought eight kids, ranging from age ten to nineteen; Emma had brought a friend. The plan was for the boys to go to the rides for the day while the girls did some serious back-to-school shopping! Since Auntie Betty had planned this with our dad, he had given her money for everything! This was a huge gift for each of us, not to mention rare! As the youngest of four, I NEVER got new clothes! Everyone's hand-me-downs, including cousins' and friends', boys' or girls', would be funnelled to me, so the idea of my very own brand-new clothes from a store I had never heard of was overwhelming.

I was speechless as I stepped inside the world's biggest mall, and I had to hold back my tears of utter joy. The rides (the boys' first stop was going to be the Drop of Doom!), the indoor skating rink, eating in a big food court—so many wonderful things were going to happen! This was the first event in my young life that felt magical. Before the boys parted ways with us, they were given clear, matter-of-fact instructions by Auntie Betty to meet us at the ice palace at 5:00 p.m. so we could all go for supper.

"Understood?" she said with serious crook of her eyebrow.

The four teenagers all knew the plan and nodded their heads.

"Make sure to check your watches so you're not late, OK?"

The boys nodded absently as they raced towards the theme park to get their day passes. It was 10:30 in the morning. The ride had been long, but the wait was over. We were actually there!

Looking to my auntie, I eagerly awaited our instructions. I saw that big pool, and as much as I wanted to go into it, I knew we would spend our time shopping. We walked over to the giant wave pool to watch. It's the most incredible pool I'd ever seen! Mind you, my comparison would be the small pool Auntie Bernice had taken us to in Choiceland, Saskatchewan.

Since Kim and I had no idea about money, Auntie Betty handled that part and made sure we didn't overspend. We ended up with what Dad requested: three pairs of pants, tops and a pair of runners each for school. I couldn't recall a time when we were ever allowed to get so many items at once! Auntie found some deals, and we were able to get a few extra pieces like a couple pairs of shorts. I bought a button-up shirt that had sliced watermelons, oranges and strawberries all over it—I loved it so much I planned to wear it for school pictures in September.

The boys were not interested in clothes, and they used their money on the Drop of Doom, the rollercoasters and snacks, and; they had an absolute blast! As we were walking to the food court to meet up with the boys for supper, I saw the skating rink right smack dab in the middle of the mall! I was in love! All I wanted to do was skate. Besides skating in phys. ed. class, Kimberley and I loved skating on frozen ponds once the snow melted enough for them to form and freeze. I had been passionate about figure skating forever (well, as long as a ten-year-old can be), and I desperately wanted lessons. Two things held my dad back from making those lessons come true: money and convenience. I was a good little skater and came by it honestly as my mom and aunts were figure skaters. We didn't have enough time for us to skate but seeing a rink the middle of a mall was pretty much the coolest thing ever!

As exhausted as I was by the end of that day, I didn't want it to end. The feelings of happiness and joy radiated from all of us, and this was a day that would forever stay etched in our minds and hearts. On our way back to my aunt's, I was excited by the idea that when we went back to school in a couple of weeks, I would have an awesome adventure to share with my classmates about my summer! All the other kids usually had stories about going to the lake and fishing to share, but our family never did stuff like that; we didn't go anywhere besides Kindersley. This year would be different. We had just made wonderful memories, ones that would top going to the lake or fishing! Even though our day at the coolest mall had ended, that thought of being able to relive it and share the story with others kept the embers of joy burning in my heart.

Chapter 10

Grandma's House

From the time I started forming memories, Grandma Kirk was always there. Her pale blue eyes were surrounded by age, and her droopy lids made her seem rather puppylike, which embedded a trusting feeling deep inside my child-size heart. Her arms were open as soon as she opened her back door and enveloped me tightly. I would smile, and she would reassure me of how loved I was. Even if she was exhausted, as she no doubt was, she was comfort, safety, stability and loving warmth for all of us. No matter how chaotic our home world became, Grandma's house was where we left those troubles behind.

After church on Sunday mornings, we went to Grandma's house for lunch. Her staple dessert was gelatin Sometimes after school we would be sent on a mission to pick up her groceries, and the best part was each getting a bit of change to buy some candy. I was partial to the fruity bubble gum, often putting all seven pieces in my little mouth at once!

When I was battling yet another excruciating ear infection, which seemed to be often, Grandma would ask me to stay the night. She'd get the hot-water bottle ready, cover me up tightly and nurse me back to health. She was our second mother, but for me, more like a first.

Sleepovers were frequent. The boys stayed in the room across the hall while Kim and I bookended Grandma. At bedtime she would softly tug the cord tethered to her bed lamp (a lamp that attached to her headboard—oh, how I wished I had one of those to read my comic books into the night!), illuminating the book of choice to be read. This simple gesture made me feel like I belonged. Nestled tightly against her withered body, I felt her strong and steady love for me.

My grandma was not a youthful woman. She was older when she had my dad, thirty-six, and my dad waited a bit longer (for his generation) to have kids as well. (By the time I arrived, Dad was closing in on his thirty-third birthday.) Grandma had a weak heart and low blood pressure, and both plagued her for years. One cold winter's evening, Dad told the four of us an amazing story about her.

"Did you know your grandmother passed away in 1970?" he asked. "The doctor said she was dead on the table. She has always had something or other—bad headaches and a weak heart. Low blood pressure was the cause of this—her weak heart."

I was on the edge of my seat as he continued.

"Grandma lay there, dead, with doctors trying to restart her heart."

Imagining this, my eyes welled up with tears. My grandma was my best friend, and I could hardly stand to hear what he was saying, but I knew I must keep listening.

"Now this is what my mother told me. She saw what happens when you die," he said. "She made it to the white gate, St. Peter greeted her. She could see her body laying on the hospital bed. She saw all the doctors and nurses frantically trying to revive the already broken heart."

My imagination was vivid, so I could see everything Dad was telling me.

"What happened next?" I said breathlessly.

"What happened next, Diana, was nothing short of a miracle! St. Peter spoke to Grandma!"

All four of us kids gasped in unison and said, "WHAT?" We exchanged smiles, delighted in this story, especially so since we were avid churchgoers who attended Plenty United Church each Sunday before eating lunch at Grandma's. We would usually spend the afternoon and well into the evening.

"When Grandma saw St. Peter at the white gate, he had a message for her: 'You must go back.' She looked back down at her lifeless body and asked, 'Why?' St. Peter then told her, 'Your job is not done yet.'

I looked at my siblings, then towards my father; I knew it was *her* job to take care of us. I knew that without Grandma around during our hardest times, those social workers that kept coming by would eventually succeed in taking us.

By the winter of 1986, shortly after grandma's eightieth birthday (I was eight), Grandma was placed in a nursing home due to failing health. Words fail to explain the ache I felt deep inside my heart. No longer was there a safe haven to go to, a place where we could be kids that helped around the house but weren't expected to do more. Gone was the makeshift grocery store she would set up for us so we could pretend to shop. She saved all kinds of food boxes—gelatin, pudding and cereal, etc.—so we could get the full experience. With Grandma in the home, the lightness in my world dimmed greatly.

Mom didn't take it well that Grandma had to go into a home either. I recall Dad saying the nursing staff at the hospital were worried about her since she wasn't eating. Dad had told her about Grandma's move, and it hurt her heart, although all the pain was stuck inside her and she was unable to share the pains of her soul verbally. Troubles between our other grandma and our dad kept my other grandparents away most of the time. When we did go there, they all smoked heavily, and with my asthma, I would end up in the hospital. It was not the best situation, and Dad kept us away even though they only lived a few miles away on a farm.

On March 23, 1987, two days after my ninth birthday and two days before Kim's eleventh, Grandma Kirk passed away. Grief and sadness enveloped our entire family. That day was the annual ski trip to our local ski hill, Twin Towers. We had spent the day before with Grandma, the hospital only allowing two of us in at a time. Dad had told me to say goodbye as I stood beside my sleeping grandma who was hooked up to all kinds of mysterious machines.

"Remember, Diana, Grandma always told me that blood is thicker than water. That means family is everything. We are blood. You have her blood in you," Dad said, staring blankly at the screens.

That comment left me very confused and a little concerned, but I didn't ask for further explanation; there are times for questions, and my intuition told me this was not one of them.

In typical nine-year-old fashion, I went barrelling through the door with my mouth going as fast as my legs! I wanted to share my exciting day with Dad.

"Skiing was so awesome, Dad! I went down Bircher Bowl superfast and I wasn't even scared!"

I rounded into the living room after dropping my bag and ski pants in the front porch.

"Dad?" I questioned as I saw him on the couch, his face stuffed into the cushions. "What's wrong?"

Dad pulled his tear-stained face away and let out a wail of emotion I had never heard before or since. I raced to his side.

"Grandma died," he said, his voice laced tight in pain.

The pain he felt could not be contained. Dad was mostly comfortable sharing anger, disappointment and frustration mixed in with some happiness, but he never showed me this side, his great sadness. I immediately joined in and began wailing. Aaron did, too, but Chris and Kimberley held it together. All I thought at that time was that my world was never going to be the same. And I was right. I had lost the person that loved me the best. I had lost my best friend.

In Grandma's home, hugs were given freely, and love was heaped on my plate along with plenty of food and fun! She took an afternoon nap but never forced me to. Rules were loose at Grandma's house, and the biggest feeling that I sensed in her home was belonging. I did not have to be a certain way in order to gain approval; I was simply and truly just me—a green/hazel-eyed little girl with a boy's haircut and a small frame who was full of light and laughter. It was safe to be a child around Grandma.

I never did ask him, but feel it's safe to say, that our father was not only grieving the loss of his mother, but he was scared to death of what was going to happen to his family without her.

During the funeral service, I sat beside my dad. I couldn't fathom how he was not crying, which is exactly what I felt like doing. At one point I looked up at him, tears brimming. He shot me a look of annoyance and said, "Don't you cry." I was shocked. Just two days before I cried freely, openly, in our home. Other than when I was in physical pain, this was the first time I was able to cry tears from the sadness I carried in front of my family. There were many other times I wanted to cry, especially over mom's sickness, but I was told not to. I had been hoping that since Dad and I cried together before that we would be free to do so again here, during her funeral. I was mistaken. Instead of letting my natural emotions out, I was forced into silent tears, crying only on the inside. Sitting in the comforts of our small United church, we were surrounded by a community of people who were left wondering what the four young Kirk kids would do now, but I did not cry in that church.

After church ended, we rode over to the graveyard, which was just outside of Plenty. It was a cold day, miserable really, which fit my mood. I had never seen an open grave, but I stood quietly as the funeral attendants moved Grandma's casket over the big hole. I didn't like this. My mind chased my thoughts, trying not to grab onto the scariest ones—the ones where I pictured Grandma's body under the ground or the people shovelling dirt over it. My mind was in absolute terror as the minister spoke his final words.

"Ashes to ashes, dust to dust."

With that, I did something I had never done before: I betrayed my dad's orders. The dam I had built to keep the tears at bay broke. I ran as fast as I could to our yellow 1983 Ford van, flung open the door and tucked myself in the back seat. I was ashamed that I couldn't keep my emotions in check as Dad had demanded, but it was an impossible task. I just cried. I ran away because I knew I would be in trouble. No one else moved from their post beside our dad. Only me.

A few minutes later, I was still unable to stuff those tears back inside myself. Auntie Bernice came to find me. It must have been a hard day for her as well, but she did something for me that helped me reckon my wounded heart. She allowed me my tears. She held me like Grandma used to and accepted me. I didn't have to pretend to be who I wasn't in order to please her. I just needed to be me. I knew this feeling would be short-lived, that I would have to fall back into order once the rest of the family made their way to the van, but for that small moment in time I felt that someone in this world knew the true me, tears and all.

After burying my grandma, a shift happened deep inside. I knew I had to step up to the plate for my family. Something else settled in my bones, too, though. I understood my father was not always right. Even though he set the rules of the house, I decided I set my pace. We settled into a very different routine, lifting heavier loads of responsibility without our security net of Grandma. Before, even when things were chaotic at home, we always knew we could depend on our love from the woman who stepped up when many others stepped—or were pushed—out. Our dad was still gone drinking, all the while a heaviness filled our house and consumed our souls. If I were to name that heartache now, I would call it grief. Back then we had no words to explain that dark place inside me. All I knew was there was no light and a hell of a lot of pain. It was as if the house breathed and bred it.

Chapter 11

Shadow Tag

Farm life and family wasn't always trauma-inducing madness. There were times filled with simple joy as the world graced us children with temporary reprieve. These were the times when us kids didn't have to be adults and worry about finances or food, caregiving or illness. We could just dance in the moonlight and shimmer in the shadows. These shadows didn't hold unknown fears, but playful fun.

We would dash in and out of the harvest moon shadows cast by the old milk barn, the bins and the other outbuildings, racing our way to "Home free!" One of us would be the catcher who romped around the yard trying to catch the others as they ducked in and out of the shadows. Making our way to safety was full of laughs and trickery! It was never easy to evade the captor, especially when the boys were chasing us! You were considered "caught" when your shadow was stepped on, so this forced you to be mindful of the direction and placement your shadow cast! Although my shadow was small, so were my legs, which made escaping the captor's line of attack difficult! The boys had notably bigger shadows. Nevertheless, this was one of my favourite family games. Even though Dad was probably not home and we were again left to our own devices, we managed to make some fun out of nothing but the moon and our imaginations.

That is what I enjoyed the most about the farm—the freedom to just be. We didn't have friends over, and Dad rarely had company other than some drinking buddies, which meant we had to make do with what we had: imagination!

Chapter 12

Need a Ride?

I liked to keep myself busy with extra-curricular activities, but there was one downside to this. Every time I needed to be picked up after school, my dad was never there because he was keeping post at the bar. Kim and I were both embarrassed about this. We would get out of volleyball practice only to be left standing in front of the school watching everyone else get picked up. At first, this was OK since our grandma lived in town and she was always home. Bouncing our way to her house was second nature and something we both enjoyed. That all changed once we no longer had her home to shelter us. It was an odd feeling to see her house standing there as it always had and know we could not seek refuge. Instead, it stood empty.

Kim and I had some good friends that lived in town, and they would usually wait with us. If he didn't show up within an hour, we'd call home or the bar from school or from their house. The biggest thing that bothered me was people knowing where he was because it clearly showed where his priorities laid. I could deal with him being drunk at home because I could hide the shame behind the four walls, but when my friends wondered why my dad wasn't there to pick us up, I didn't know what to say. I wonder what the conversation was after we left their house when he finally arrived to take us home. I am sure they would question their parents after the tenth time Kim and I were not picked up on time.

There was, however, times when my friends had places to be and couldn't wait with me. When I was at an after-school activity that Kim wasn't part of, I would wait alone outside even though the school was not locked. The last teacher of the day or the janitor would usually ask if my dad was coming to pick me up, so I would make some sort of excuse as to why he was late and then watch them drive away.

There were times, however, when it was freeze-your-blood-to-your-bones cold outside, so I would make my way to where I knew Dad would be: the Plenty Hotel. I remember one time when it was so cold out that I had to find him before I froze to death. I kept my head down as I walked into the icy prairie wind towards the bar, chin tucked into my mint green winter coat. The challenge was keeping my glasses from frosting up, so I lifted my head up and turned myself around to walk backwards and cut the wind. This allowed my glasses to defog enough for me to see. Of course, I had to peer backwards a few times to catch the end of the sidewalk and navigate myself safely off the edge to cross the road.

Upon reaching the bar, I saw our bright yellow van parked out front where it was most nights of the week: squarely in front of the front door. I figured I could have crawled inside and at the very least been protected from the harsh Saskatchewan elements. As I approached, I felt the elated feeling of safety within reach. Best of all, I could continue to hide my dad's drinking and how bad the neglect had gotten. I didn't want the social workers to come back, and I didn't want anyone to see me and report my dad. I also didn't want to be blamed if our family was broken up by the social workers. After all, I was already the cause of Mom's illness.

I reached for the silver door handle and pulled it towards me—it wouldn't budge. It was locked. I rounded the van to the driver's door and tried it, but it was locked too.

"Surely the side door or back will open," I thought out loud, the words whispered from my lips into the wind.

I was wrong again. I was completely locked out. Dad was paranoid about people stealing his things, often accusing "friends" of taking gas or tools when we weren't home. Whenever Dad was ranting about some friend stealing something, I quietly thought maybe he should get new friends! I felt defeated and stood outside that van for what felt like forever. My toes began to numb as the cold winter settled beneath my skin. I thought about going back to the school, but it was getting late, the janitor would be leaving soon, and I wanted to save myself a bit of humiliation. The wind continued to howl as my mind figured out what to do.

The thought crossed my mind to go into the bar and just ask Dad to unlock the van. Clearly, he was right there, only a few yards away from me, but he had no idea I was outside those doors that always welcomed him and his money. Instead, I allowed my fear to dictate my decision-making rather than listening to my rational side that knew what I needed to do. I decided not to go back to the school grounds, and I waited outside the entrance where there was a bit of shelter. I decided against going into the bar to ask for the van keys because I feared it may rile up the angry beast to the point where I would regret showing my face where I knew it was illegal. So, at ten years old, I did the only thing I saw as practical: I crouched in the back doorway area, the one that was rarely used, and hid myself as best I could from the wind, snow and people. I did not want to be seen by anyone driving by. What if one of my friends was with their parents and drove by to see me buried against the front door of the bar? That would be terribly embarrassing.

If I heard the door, I would peer through the corner of the building to see if it was Dad. I waited outside for what felt like hours—I can't say for sure how long—while the snow piled up around my little body. The cement I was sitting on created a chill that hurt my bones, but I kept myself busy with thoughts of how he would react to having me there, and the fear kept me warm.

By the time Dad came out, I had lost track of time. I walked around the corner just in time to see him turning the key to unlock the door. I pretended I had just walked from the school and made my way inside. No questions were asked. My snow-covered and shaky body were not inspected. Dad did not know I had spent the last few hours in the cold.

After I got home, I went straight to my room. Aaron knew something was off, and he was clearly upset when he came into my bedroom where Kim and Chris were already checking on me. He said Dad had been gone for hours, and I was due home so they had been worried we had hit the ditch with all the snow. I told them what happened, and that is when Aaron gave me a piece of advice I would use every time going forward.

"Go to the church basement," he said. "The church is never locked. It's warm, you'll be safe there."

That is just what I did from then on. As awkward and scared as I felt to go even there, I knew it would be a safe and warm place. Aaron and Chris must have told Dad I would be at the church as he somehow knew to pick me up there.

No one should ever feel that unwanted. Not being chosen, not being worthy, not being good enough puts something into my mind that took decades to remove. Being forgotten embedded a deep need to be seen in me, but I also knew that would not be possible for my dad. All he could see was the bleak hopelessness that pervaded our home.

On the upside, this parental neglect embedded a deep love for my siblings and a knowing that no matter what the world brought us, no matter if our own father did not have our backs much of the time, that we would be there for one another. No matter where we went in life, the foundations set in childhood would sustain us as adults. The comfort of knowing that very thing helped fill the void of pain that rejection and illness opened. My parents didn't come in conventional forms, but the love of a circle of people who I knew I could trust with my life saved me. They always had my back.

Chapter 13

Birthday Season

March 21 kicked off a special time in the Kirk household each year: birthday season! Five out of six birthdays took place between the kick-off date, my birthday, and April 13, Chris's birthday. Kim and I were just days apart—hers was on the March 25. It was often joked that it was calving season since we were all born so closely together!

Kim and I often shared a cake. It was okay, but it also sparked the debate as to when to do the actual celebrating. It wasn't something I paid much attention to until I was older. Mostly we celebrated whenever it worked out, pictures would be taken of us with our cake and life would go on. I knew we were lucky to have such a luxury, so complaining was not on my mind. When we got old enough to help out with the groceries, we would pick up enough cake mixes so everyone could have their own. We each picked out our favourite Duncan Hines along with some icing sugar and eggs. Sometimes we even splurged on some food colouring, which Kim and I found more uses for than just icing.

Kim always knew her presents when I opened mine as Dad would buy two of the same items, usually in different colours. This also made hand-me-downs pretty boring. I would wear the same thing for two or three years. For the most part, he treated us as twins even though we were two years apart. I suppose it was simply easier, faster and required less thinking.

On my tenth and Kim's twelfth birthdays we were treated to our first ever birthday party! Excitement filled our hearts and the house in anticipation of balloons, cakes and, most importantly, friends coming over! Hanging out with friends at our house rarely happened. Our auntie Gracie asked Dad if she could make us cakes and throw a party for us; she would take care of everything! Dad thought it was a nice idea and knew it would warm his little daughters' hearts, so the birthday party was set and planned!

Sitting through school all day long was torture! My wiggly mind wandered constantly to what festivities lay ahead for us. Surprises of a good nature were few and far between in our house, so this was particularly special. When the dismissal bell rang at 3:15, Kim and I each gathered up our friends to bring them home with us on the school bus. I was kept from sleep the night before wondering who would sit with me; maybe we could fit three to a seat if the bus driver allowed.

The excitement built as we filed onto the bright yellow bus with our friends. Much to my relief, both of my friends were able to sit with me. We were off second on the bus route, so the ride was quick, which was all the better for six anxious girls!

When we walked into the house, an energy of happiness and excitement was in the air. Festive balloons and streamers lined the halls, aunt Gracie quickly ushered us all to the table for a quick snack. Giggles and games were soon well underway, and Dad even picked up Mom from the hospital for the day. I could see that Mom felt the same excited energy as us as she wore a big smile and let squeals of glee escape her mouth as we all ran around chasing each other and playing Pin the Tail on the Donkey.

Supper was a childhood staple: hotdogs! Once again, we filed towards the dining room table to eat. Mom was in her wheelchair with her table fastened tightly to the arms, allowing her meal to sit in front of her. Our caregiver Dean was there, feeding Mom the hotdog. I was mid-bite when the commotion started. Mom was choking. All of us backed away as the adults tried to dislodge a piece of hotdog stuck in Mom's airway. A silent panic swept the room, no one sure what to do. Dad yelled for us to go up to our room, but I stood there, frozen, while the other kids moved quickly up the stairs. Mom wasn't breathing, and I was terrified.

Dean laid her down, but this did not help, so aunt Gracie jumped in, knowing every second counted. I scurried up the stairs to my bedroom where my friends had converged, scared and quiet, flung open my closet doors and tucked myself away in the back cubby. This was the place I went when I was afraid. This is where I thought fear could not get me, but I was enwrapped in terror. My friends quickly followed me into the closet. Tears erupted, but words did not. They sat with me until Aaron knocked on the door and gave a full report. Mom was okay. Aunt Gracie had wrapped her arms around Mom and thrust her fists into her ribcage. After a few attempts, the hotdog was dislodged and Mom could breathe.

I looked around the room at my friends, seeing and feeling the fear dissipate from their faces, but I was still very upset. I knew our life with a sick mother was different than most. It was plain to see we were not like the rest of the small-town families, but today I desperately wanted things to be "normal," yet they weren't. Guilt surfaced at my own selfish anger. I didn't want to be mad at Mom for choking—people choke all the time. But in our lives, Mom choked regularly, each time leaving a slight cut of fear and panic on my heart. I didn't want my friends to see this side of our life. I wanted to be accepted like everyone else.

Shortly after supper we gathered up our friends to drop them off. Kim's friends were being taken home by Aunt Gracie and mine by Dad. Choking exhausted Mom and scared Dad, so he felt it best to take her back to the hospital. When he arrived back home, I could smell the familiar aroma of beer, a scent I had grown used to on him. My friends piled in the van. We dropped off Lindsay first, then went over to Mauri's, then Jodi was the last one off as she lived right in Plenty. After they were all at home, Dad pulled up in front of the familiar large brown building on Main Street—the Plenty Hotel. I wondered what we were doing there when Dad slipped the keys from the ignition and slid them into his pocket. He grabbed the handle of the door while turning back towards me.

"I'll just be a few minutes."

I sat in the darkness of March, waiting. Looking towards the streetlight on the corner I could see sparkles of snow dancing in the air. The cold of winter filled the van. With no keys, I could not start it to warm myself up. It was getting so cold, and I chastised myself for not putting on my ski pants. I wanted to appear cool to my friends, and now I literally was.

Frost started drawing across the windows as the night carried on. I diligently worked to keep myself warm with memories of earlier that day playing in my mind like a movie. I wondered if Kim had made it back home. I wondered if my siblings knew where I was, if they knew how cold it was or how much snow we were getting. Mostly, I wondered why my dad was in the bar and not taking me home. I wondered why he didn't care enough about me to check on me and see if I was okay.

Minutes turned to hours as I froze in our van like a little popsicle. I was certain my toes were blue. I was huddled up in the back of the van, curled up on the velvet seats trying to use the brown velvety curtain as a blanket when I heard the squeak of the driver's side door. It was Dad, finally. He didn't say anything and neither did I. I wanted to yell at him, to tell him I was frozen, scream at him for ruining what was supposed to be a great day for me! Instead, we let the silence fall between us as Dad navigated the old snow-covered highway back to the farm. I was too afraid of him to let out my hurt, my anger, my pain, so I did what we had been taught to do. I swallowed it all.

Chapter 14

Imagination

Spring on the farm was simply a beautiful time of year. Slowly, the thick white blanket of snow would melt and reveal all the treasure it hid for the previous five months. Suddenly, and with seamless effort, Mother Nature would remind me of all the good in our world with the stunning beauty of a prairie sky during the rise and fall of the sun. Of course, those sunrises and sunsets happened and were beautiful in the long Saskatchewan winter, too, but with the dawn of spring and the sun rising earlier and staying up later, somehow our eyes came into focus a little bit more. We saw what was already there, but feeling the warmth meant we could feel hope. While the sun of the winter is bright and brilliant, it lacks the warmth we needed to feel closer to it. Plus, the dark nights made it feel like winter would never end.

Kim and I would strap on our skates in the early mornings when the sloughs were still frozen and practice our waltz jumps, spirals and toe loops. Neither one of us had still not taken a skating lesson, but we watched enough of it on TV that we figured we knew what we were doing. We would make up routines, each of us taking turns showcasing our skills while the other sat on the edge of the slough in the snow. Often, I would dream of being part of the local skating club and participating in their annual carnival. I loved the pretty dresses and fancy hair and makeup. In my mind, I wasn't a half bad skater either. Our dreams of skating on the ice stage at the carnival would never be realized, so the slough south of the yard and audience of vehicles passing by would be the only stage we had. Walking from the farmhouse to the ice, toe picks poking our backs as we dreamed of having skate guards like all the real skaters did, was what we got. We knew better not to ask. Mom's sickness was aggressive, and she was deteriorating fast. The last thing our dad needed or wanted to hear from me was my wants or needs. I had to do what I could to help out and fly under the radar. After all, this illness was all my fault.

My favourite time of year was when the fruit trees and lilacs were in full bloom. Kim often shared her daydreams with me. One sunny late spring afternoon, we went out for a walk, bright colours of the blossoms enticing us towards them.

"Diana, I can see it now. Imagine standing right here," she said, planting herself squarely between two blossoming, deep purple lilac bushes. Her arms were spread wide as she showed me her thoughts on her wedding. "See? Guests can sit here. I don't want a big wedding; something small with our close family and friends. If you're not too big of a jerk, maybe you can be my maid of honour."

At eight and ten years old, we were a long way from getting married, but it was certainly fun to pass the long days daydreaming.

In the summer of 1987, Chris, Kim and I decided to make a fort out of railway ties. There was a short rail line a quarter of a mile north of our family farm. Sometimes they had to replace the wood (ties) which secured the train tracks. They stacked the old wood beside the train tracks for the company to collect, but these ties remained where they were stacked most of the time as they were of no further use to the rail company. Railway ties were about 7" x 9" and eight feet long with an average weight of about two hundred pounds, so you can see why the rail line wasn't too keen on picking up miles upon miles of them. Locals capitalized on this and brought them home for various uses. One thing I learned about living on the farm was that there was always more than one use for an item; all you needed was a little imagination.

Dad framed out a flower bed in the front yard right in front of our deck, but there were many left over that sat beside our Quonset, stacked nicely in rows. None of us inquired about any further plans Dad had with these. All we needed was a child's imagination, and we knew we would come up with something.

I was all of ten years old when Chris—whose grand ideas and designs entertained us for hours—got a big idea.

"Let's build the biggest and best fort we can!" he said. "This isn't going to be any regular fort, no way! It will be two stories, with a rope or ladder to get to the second floor! This is going to make Aaron's fort look small!"

There was always a competition between Aaron and Chris for Dad's attention, and Chris was sure he'd come out from Aaron's shadow with this one. He had no idea how true this was.

"We can make curtains out of some old sheets!" I chimed excitedly.

"Yeah, yeah, sure Diana," Chris agreed. "Guess what we're going to use to make the fort out of?"

Looking around, Kim and I shrugged our shoulders in unison.

"We give up! What?" Kim piped up.

"We are going to make this fort out of all those railway ties Dad has sitting by the Quonset."

Shocked, Kim and I deflated slightly.

"Chris, that is crazy! There is no way we can do that!" I reasoned. "Do you know how heavy those things are?"

Had he forgotten that Kim and I were just scrawny little girls? How would we lift those railway ties when our combined weight, including Chris, was probably not even 250 pounds?

"Trust me, girls, we can do this. I'll be on one end and you two on the other. We will figure it out. I can almost carry them by myself, but it will be too hard to put get them up to the second story without you guys! Come on, let's build an awesome fort that we can all hang out in!"

If we knew anything about Chris, it was that he was a smooth salesman. Kim and I were slinging those railway ties with Chris and building the coolest fort we had ever seen! Slow and steady we moved each railway tie into position, Kim and I on one end while Chris took the other. It took a few days, from sunup to sundown. We normally spent most of our time outdoors, but this place would offer a cool refuge from the house on days it was raining and we didn't want to be inside. We talked of maybe not letting Aaron into the fort, as he was trying to make his cooler than ours. I secretly felt bad for him, but I wasn't about to switch teams when we clearly had the better fort.

We helped ourselves to as many ties as needed to complete our project. The design and layout were shocking and impressive—not only to us but to our father as well. He was undoubtedly surprised, but there was one small yet important detail we had gotten all wrong: location. In order to keep our project a surprise, we built the fort behind the Quonset, the building that housed most of Dad's farm equipment. There was a set of large doors at the front and the back of the building, and our masterpiece was located directly behind the back set of doors. Dad usually used the front doors to move equipment in and out, but he also needed access to the back. Much to our disappointment, and also our dad's, he told us we would not be able to keep it where it was. Tie by tie, we pulled apart all our hard work, vowing to rebuild it in a better location. We didn't, though. We lost our excitement, and soon all that was left was the knowing that when you put your mind to something—no matter how out of reach the project looks and no matter your size—if you believe you can do it, you will. That fort taught us that this world is really only limited by what we *think* we can or cannot do.

Chapter 15

The Drought of '88

The sweltering heat of the summer of 1988 made it unbearable in a house that wasn't air conditioned. Mom was still in Dodsland Hospital, losing ground quickly to this nameless illness. Dad took to closet drinking, and we had a new caregiver, a university student who was paying her way through teaching school; we were her summer job. At ten years old, I was still quite into playing with Barbie dolls, and sewing Barbie clothes and playing dolls were just a couple of the things she filled our days with.

However, there was a notable difference this year; the stress of the farm showed more in Dad's actions. Rain wasn't coming like years previous, and we were in the middle of the driest year since the Dirty Thirties. The salt lake several miles from our farm had dried up, and with the wind blowing strong, the salt found its way into our house if we didn't shut the windows tight. When the windows had been left open during the day, we could write our names in the salt on our antique oak kitchen table. It left a fine layer on everything it contacted, including my tongue.

If you aren't familiar with the Saskatchewan prairie, it's pretty desolate, trees are sparse, and it looks more like a desert during a drought. The air became heavy with heat and dust which scorched the thirsty ground. Cracks in the clay soil grew larger by the day, which I really didn't mind as it was interesting to investigate what was living among them. I usually saw the black crickets crawl in an out of those big, long cracks like they had somewhere important to be.

At night, I would open my upstairs bedroom window to get some reprieve from the slow cooker of a farmhouse. I liked my bedroom upstairs, and Kim's was across the hall near the bathroom. Many times, we would push our beds into each other's rooms. On those sweltering prairie nights with the window wide open, it was as if breath came back into the old, towering farmhouse; what was once contracted, opened and surrendered to the joyous reprieve from sunshine and heat. I would fall asleep to the gentle soft songs those busy little crickets serenaded us with each nightfall. Their soothing songs lulled my worried heart to sleep.

The heat baked everything. Crops that had been planted in April and May were not popping out of the ground, and by mid-July, when they should be lavishly green and filling with grains, the seeds sat docile in the dust. Driving along the gravel roads, you had to hang back, away from the vehicle in front of you as the dust cloud made it so you couldn't see if there was any oncoming traffic. The pavement melted before your very eyes, and thick, black tar rose like steam from a thawing lake on a bright spring day. Looking north from my second-story bedroom window towards the fields, waves of heat danced against the glistening sunlight. The fields were baron prairie terrain, dark and dank. I didn't understand why I couldn't take the garden hose out there and water the crops and was heckled by my brothers for thinking so foolishly. The mind of a ten-year-old girl was too far out of reach from those teenage boy brains full of girls and farm knowledge.

Apparently, the ground wasn't the only thing that was suffering a drought. Dad's bank account was as dry as a bone too. Ask any farmer in Saskatchewan about the drought of '88, and they will tell you stories of how many farmers were forced to sell out or had the banks foreclose on them. This pushed them to the city where they could obtain steady employment and feed their families. Others, such as our dad, had to negotiate with the bank just to keep the land he already had. I didn't really understand how money worked as a kid—heck, sometimes I don't as an adult—but I knew that kids who had been in school with me were moving, and that made me sad.

In 1987, my dad purchased the land next to the railroad tracks. It was one quarter north of the home quarter, and it cost a lot, but he hoped the extra income from it would put us in a better financial situation. This was a gamble, and if I knew anything about my dad in his younger days, he was a risk-taker. It was either going to pay off and put him ahead or bust him. A drought was the last thing anyone needed at the time, but especially Dad, a single father with little support.

He struggled to recover from that 1988 drought. We were no longer in need of caregivers, which was probably just as well, as dad wouldn't have been able to afford one anyway. His pocketbook was skinny.

Aaron was sixteen and old enough to drive, and the change in the household was notable, even at my age. Groceries became our duty as kids. Aaron would load us all in his car he bought with money he had saved from working for a neighbour as a farmhand, and we would make a weekly trip into town to the Lucky Dollar, the only grocery store in Plenty. I knew we could only afford the basics: milk, bread, cheese slices, eggs, bacon, margarine, cereal, apples, lunch meat and maybe pudding cups for our lunches. I hungrily eyed the chips, crisp in bags tightly nestled together atop a wire shelf. I would wander over to the pop, thinking of how much Mom loved Coke and longing to feel the powerful, eye-burning rich goodness encapsulated within the glassy bottle.

There were occasions where we planned meals, such as pizza. On these days we were allowed to purchase a brick of cheese along with a pizza kit. Somehow, I managed to consistently get stuck on dough duty while everyone else had jobs where they could eat their product. It was a boxed pizza mix, so we just had to add water and mix it all up then knead it and let it rise with a towel over it—a trick I had seen Dean use when waiting for bread or bun dough to rise. Chris would get the big green and white cheese grater machine Mom got as a shower gift out. It had a crank and plate attachments so you could slice potatoes and do many things with it, but to us it was the fancy cheese grater saved especially for pizza night!

I remember browsing the aisles of Smith's Lucky Dollar one time when I spied something I really wanted: an *Archie* comic. They were seventy-five cents, and sometimes Dad would buy them for me. Aaron would not, and I knew I would be out of luck that day. As if reading my mind, Aaron looked down, catching me longingly staring at the latest edition.

"Looks like Archie may finally be with Betty," I mumbled without thinking.

Aaron met my eyes, and I saw how sad he was.

"Not today, Diana."

I put it down and stared at the bill in front of us on the counter: $839.84. Our dad had a charge account at the grocery store, and sometimes we would bring in cheques to pay things down, but today we had nothing. The storekeeper was a round and happy man with stout legs. He mentioned, rather awkwardly, that he would need a payment next time we were in. Aaron's face reddened as he nodded. I saw the long list of charges written neatly on the right column of the charge card. Embarrassment found my cheeks as well, and nestled in my mind as I panicked. I wondered if we would be able to bring the food home or if we would starve. The cupboards currently had corn starch, salt and pepper, dried lentils, coconut, powdered milk cream of wheat and oatmeal. The milk was near empty, and there was a can of opened beans with some plastic wrap on them, a few eggs, the ends of bread tucked in the bag as if hiding themselves so we are not interested in eating them, and some mustard. We needed this food.

Aaron sensed my anxiousness and looked at me with reassurance, silently telling me we would be okay. It was a look I knew well. The nice man allowed us to charge what we needed without having to put things back, and I sighed in relief. At that moment, I was grateful for where we lived, grateful for our small-town grocery store and grateful for Aaron's penny pinching. It was worse to feel the pains of hunger than the pains of not getting a comic. I could read the ones I had. The thought that pressed forward in my mind, though, was this: we were poor.

Chapter 16

The Silence

The daily visits to see Mom turned into every second day, and then weekly. Mom had to be moved to Kerrobert for her care because they closed the hospital in Dodsland. Kerrobert was a half hour away instead of the ten-minute drive to Dodsland, and we all felt the distance it created.

Mom could either be found in her shared hospital room or the tv room. Her room was plain white, and a thin white curtain was usually tucked neatly against the wall and was only pulled if Mom had a roommate. Each time I walked inside the hospital, my nose reminded me of the familiarity of this place – the scent being my strongest tie to bring forth the pictures locked away in memory. Mom's bed was tucked by the window which backed on some trees and grass. It was not a fancy view, but it was nice. The first thing I would do when I visited was rifle through her bedside table to find her glasses. She often couldn't keep her glasses on her face because her limbs involuntarily moved and knocked them off. We lovingly teased her about it all the time. Sometimes she would be in the TV room watching *Another World*. Her glasses had usually fallen off and her eyes were poor, so she was more listening to it, or so I thought.

The doctors had only minimally investigated this disease. In 1986, Mom was taken to Saskatoon for an MRI and some muscle studies. The disease remained without a name or a family history.

The doctors were baffled. Dad received a letter from a neurologist that said there was no funding to research the illness and no chance of her children getting it, so the affliction was allowed to progress without further investigation.

Mom began to have small seizures that graduated to grand mal, which scared me. When we first visited her, she showed her excitement through a series of noises which could be deciphered as glee! It was music to my ears. I loved seeing a big smile spread across her face. However, as the disease progressed, her excitement dissipated and her face ceased to light up. I didn't understand at the time, but some of this was the illness and the other element was the heavy dose of Valium they gave her.

Eventually, going to see Mom took on a different meaning for me. I was used to her not being able to talk, so I filled the silence with stories and adventures of what was going on in life. I was often confused as to how I really felt. Mom was a breathing body, a soul trapped inside brokenness. I had no idea what she could comprehend and what she couldn't. I didn't know if she could hear me or sense my touch, but I never gave that much thought. I focused on the senses I thought might work. I knew I was missing a bond with her that should have been sealed in my first few years of life but wasn't. I wanted to wedge my way into her soul so she knew me and looked at me with adoration and love, but it wasn't to be. That missing piece has taken a lifetime to reconcile.

When I walked the long hall to her room, my emotions were a mix of excitement to see her and sadness at knowing what I would see. I longed for the situation to be anything but what it was. I wanted her to hold me, to reach out for my touch. I wished for a hug and a soft kiss on my forehead from when I was a child and into my teenage years. The daydreams did not change. *What would I do if Mom whispered "I love you" in my ear when I leaned over to give her a hug?*

Occasionally, a resident would wander into her room, confused, mistaking the rooms. Perhaps they were lonely so they sought comfort in the sound of young voices full of stories and followed their ears to our mom's room. I don't really know, but I felt compassion for those who didn't have anyone visit them. It didn't matter if we could not enjoy the art of conversation with Mom because we could enjoy the time. Love like our mom's was not bound by words, no; we felt it in our souls. I took what I could feel from her, not what couldn't be said, and this gift has served me well. So much of our communication was in the silence, the unsaid, the wordless vibe that encompassed her world but most people learned to ignore. The true communication of the human spirit comes from the dance our souls do alone and together.

Sometimes I wondered if she was stuck between two worlds—the one here on earth and the other in heaven. Mystery surrounded every facet of this illness, and it left more questions than answers.

Chapter 17

Looking for Love on the Prairies

I was in Grade 6 when Dad attempted dating. He was forty-four and lonely. By this time, Mom had been sick for twelve years, in care for five and continuing to decline. Most of her cerebral functions were completely compromised. I never wanted to lose my belief that one day God would somehow divinely intervene, gifting Mom and her family back the life we all quietly wished for.

Sometimes he would say things like, "You kids need a mother." The idea dazzled me. I would lay on my bed for hours wondering what having a "mother" would be like. Would she cook for us and clean so we didn't have to? Would she move in and start bossing us around? Maybe we would have long talks about important things like boys and girl stuff. She could teach me how to dress nicely and apply makeup properly! The idea of Dad dropping me, Kim and "new mom" off at the Kindersley mall so we could do mother/daughter things left me breathless with excitement!

Perhaps most importantly, I would have someone to take to the Mother's Day tea at church. Kim and I were part of the United Church group called Explorers, and we hosted a Mother's Day tea each year. Aunty Betty (Mom's sister) and Grandma Cormack attended a few times, and Kim and I took great pride in showing them off like prized possessions. Then there were other times we had no one. Someone always took pity on us and offered to share their mom. The gesture was full of kindness, but I never got used to walking into the basement of our beautiful church knowing our own mother would not be there. Kim and I would sit together and wait for someone to look our way and "adopt" us into their family table, but it made me feel like I didn't fit in even more so. There was also the fact that we could never hide this, which is something we both wanted to do. We were comfortable pretending that no one knew of our circumstances at home. Thoughts and wishes of a healthy mom danced in my mind and heart daily, but sitting on a cold wood chair in our Sunday best, doilies placed elegantly throughout the church basement, there was no hiding. Mom would not bounce down the stairs in a pretty dress, hair perfected, smile painted in red. She would not laugh and chat with all the other mothers who were her friends and old classmates. No. Our reality was much different, and the yearly public display was difficult.

Having said that, there were a few people in the community of Plenty that always ensured we felt accepted and loved on hard days. Many of my classmate's mothers went to school with my mom. I did not know this as they did not frequent our home, and mom could not speak or share stories of her own childhood friends. My parents did not have an active social life from what I recall. Mom's siblings would be over, or their parents, but no friends came to visit or help out. Sometimes, however, I would get glimpses into our parent's past. Today, I would be gifted just that by a classmate's mother, Nola. Nola was Mauri's mom. She was a cute, small woman with a heart as big as could be.

"She was quiet, always kind." Nola shared.

Our gift at that Mother's Day Tea was held in the memories Nola shared of the woman that gave me life, but I hardy knew, let alone understood.

Most everyone could go home that night, and all the other nights, to their families, to their moms. Mother's Day was the day that all the other moms and daughters felt the sting we felt each and every morning we woke: our mother would not be coming home to join the family. As much as they made an effort to help us fit in, we painfully knew we would always be the family that didn't. Fitting in wasn't part of our childhood. When you grow up in a very small, tight-knit community, the slightest imperfections can be magnified and judgement freely doled out in our direction. There were some people that held compassion for us, such as moments at the Mother's Day Tea, but generally, due to our situation, we were the easy target of gossip. Maybe Dad's mission to find us a mother would help us find our place.

I figured having a mother would change our world dramatically and in ways I knew I could not fathom. The thing is, I pretended I knew what I was missing, but my version of a typical mother was a collection of other people's relationships with their own and whatever television taught me. I would listen to my friends complain that their mom wasn't letting them do this or that, that their moms were strict and unfair. I supposed some of that to be true but also had a deep knowledge that there was far more benefit than the alternative.

I now see that, as much as Dad wanted to have a partner, he wanted someone to mother us and share his heavy load. He didn't make it about him being lonely or needing someone to love or love him back. No, it was about us and our need of a feminine influence, someone to teach his daughters how to be responsible, good women. The only bit of advice Dad preached to us girls was to "marry rich." I understand now that it stemmed from his own financial inadequacies that he didn't want for his daughters; he wanted to ensure a sound financial future for us. It struck me as strange that he did not seem to think women had a responsibility to their partner, to bring home some money and help the family financially as well. In Grade 6, I decided that one day I would have a career. I wasn't sure what it would be—heck, I wasn't sure we would have food from day to day—but I did know I would be independent. I didn't like feeling helpless and at the mercy of other people's agendas. I needed my own space, my own money, and to depend on myself. I knew it could take me a long time to achieve this seemingly ludicrous dream, but I believed I could. So yes, maybe we did need a mother, but my dad needed a partner far more.

The way my dad went about finding us a mother and himself a life partner was fairly unconventional for a farmer on the Saskatchewan prairie in early nineties. Long before the technology revolution of internet dating, options were slim. Single women in their thirties and forties were few and far between in our small town and the surrounding farming area. Most of those women were already married with established families, so the likelihood of meeting someone in the local post office, grain elevator or the bar was low. There was one lady—my friend's single mom who was rather striking—and the idea of us being sisters tickled me! We could share a room, talk all night long and then go to school together. I saw no downside, but our parents didn't run in the same social circles, so getting them together was difficult. We managed to have her mom pick her up from a sleepover a few times, and they had coffee together, but nothing ever materialized.

We were two hours west of Saskatoon, so very rural, but even though the options were limited, Dad was not deterred. He used *The Western Producer*, which was published Canada-wide. I imagine how his ad may have read: "Lonely farmer looking for love and a mother to my four young children. Serious inquires only." I don't know what the ad read, but we knew he placed it.

Imagine what the first meeting would have been like.

"Are you divorced?"

"No."

"Widowed?"

"Nope."

As far as baggage, Dad's was somewhat hefty. He would have to tell them that his wife was terminal, non-verbal, in a home. Oh, and he had four little kids and a farm. All of this information would be dumped out readily, I would think, perhaps on the first date, although I never asked. For a shy man such as Dad, this must have been putting himself out there in a way he was not accustomed to. Dad sometimes shared what he was looking for in a woman. He was big on looks, so she had to be attractive. "Classy" was another requirement, but I wasn't too sure what that meant. Dad said it was in the way she treated herself and others. Someone with a good job, perhaps a teacher. Being a farmer meant a fluctuating, unsteady income that was weather-dependent.

He must have gotten a few responses, and he met one lady for supper in Rosetown one summer evening. They had supper a few more times, but it never developed into anything.

Then he met Mary, a teacher from the Saskatoon area who was a little older and had one grown child. Dad didn't tell us right away because he probably didn't want to introduce anyone unless he felt it was going somewhere.

My dad and I were close at this time; he confided in me things he hadn't told my siblings. I don't know why, but I figured it was because I listened and may have been more open-minded than the others. When he approached the subject of dating, I was totally supportive. Aaron and Kim were leery of Dad dating because he was still married to Mom. Chris seemed to side with me, not wanting Dad to be alone forever. I guess everyone figured it would fizzle out once she discovered his drinking, but, surprisingly, Mary either did not know of my his drinking problem or she looked passed it. Dad constantly bragged about her being a schoolteacher. Many of my grandma's sisters were teachers, as was my Auntie Bernice, and this was a coveted title in my dad's eyes; the epitome of success. He would mention that she made good money and had to be accruing a good pension. I had no idea or interest in that, but I could see that financial stability in a woman was important since he could not offer that.

The first time we met Mary, she had been dating my dad for a few months, and she came to the farm for a visit. Dad had us on another cleaning frenzy; it seemed the only time we really had to clean like crazy was when company was coming over. Rooms were spotless and bathrooms scrubbed when Mary arrived in her little "pony," a small car that was apparently a classic. Dad was clean-shaven except for his mustache, which was trimmed. He wore a nice sweater he had bought on one of the many trips he had made to see Mary in Saskatoon.

I stood at the top of the wheelchair ramp on the front step, waiting. When they greeted each other, they exchanged a warm embrace and a kiss. Dad kissing someone was something I'd never seen. They seemed happy. Strangely, it didn't bother me. My siblings quickly joined me on the step, and Dad hollered, "Kids, come meet Mary!" I could hear his smile.

There is something about my personality that is not fearful, and leadership comes naturally. As the youngest, I fell to the back of the line for the longest time. However, that all changed when Grandma passed away. We had lost our matriarch and Mom was in the hospital full time, so it was up to either Kimberley or me to step up and do the cooking and cleaning. Thankfully, we had different strengths. I was the cook and Kim cleaned, although she did most of her cleaning in her bedroom and didn't really care about what the rest of the house looked like. When I needed her to help me with the rest of the housework, she was there. Aaron taught me how to make all kinds of dishes and silently passed me the responsibility of the kitchen. This freed him up to help Dad on the farm, which Chris had also been doing. Everyone had a position. Farming was a lifestyle, and we did what we had to. We weren't being shuffled to hockey games or skating practices. We were learning to navigate and survive our world and assume our new positions as parents to each other. So I took the lead as we walked out to meet Mary.

She was short, and her brown hair was done up in a fancy twist that I immediately liked. When she smiled, she had a gap between her two front teeth, also just like me! She wore glasses and dressed well, which I also liked. In a burst of pride Dad rarely showed, he introduced us and shared a bit about what we did for the family.

"Diana is a pretty good cook already, even at eleven; she will make a good wife to someone one day," he said.

That compliment had me beaming with pride.

"Aaron here likes farming, and Chris keeps the yard looking good. Both boys are pretty handy. Kim here, she's very clean."

Hearing our dad (somewhat) brag about us was strange because he was usually doling out heck to one of us for one reason or another, so this was new. A nice new. If anything, I think we enjoyed Mary just a little bit more because she had cast a spell over our dad. He was no longer yelling out orders or drunk when she was around the house.

Dad's happy-go-lucky demeanour continued as his relationship with Mary progressed. Soon, he was also picking up new hobbies such as going to garage sales. He always enjoyed auctions, and he found the same excitement in a good garage sale steal.

Their relationship continued for a number of years, and Mary became a staple in our family but remained somewhat distant. Dad met her in Saskatoon most of the time, and once Aaron moved to the city for university, Dad would stay at his place to save on hotel bills. Aaron moved into the upstairs apartment of a house Mary owned while he attended the University of Saskatchewan for agriculture. Once he was in the city, we would come into the city, which was a whole new experience for us. Before that, we only went to Kindersley or to visit family near Lloydminster. There was one trip to Edmonton and one to Calgary, but that was the extent of our travels.

Saskatoon offered some cool options for us. I enjoyed window shopping with Kim, Dad and Mary, and she commented that she had never seen kids not ask for anything when out shopping; she was impressed! I wanted some new things, but I also knew we had no money, so asking seemed pointless. The one store we went to that Mary liked was a second-hand store. Dad bought me a Sun Ice ski jacket, which was great as I still loved skiing. It wasn't in style anymore, but the brand was right and it was in perfect condition. Kim got a nice white winter jacket which looked really nice on her frail and slender build.

On the weekends we were left at the farm alone, my brothers would go out with their friends to parties and Kim and I would either spend time with our friends or hang out with each other at home watching *Unsolved Mysteries*. I can still hear Robert Stack telling our young, impressionable ears: "Maybe you can help solve a mystery!" I certainly hoped we wouldn't see anyone we knew on there.

Mary lit up our father's life. Dad became lighthearted, and he joked and laughed more than I had ever seen. He even changed how he dressed, giving up his green farmer clothing purchased at Peavey Mart for a nice pair of pants and sweater he and Mary had picked out together. He was modern, and the transformation was both unexpected and welcomed!

Besides Dad being happy, there was another upswing to their relationship: Dad would bring groceries home in bulk! We had never eaten so well! Giant double chocolate muffins packaged by the dozen, tubs of margarine larger than I had ever seen, loaves upon loaves of McGavin's bread and sometime a whole pail of bubblegum! Treats were usually limited to Sundays after visiting Mom. Dad would drive us up to the local Chinese restaurant in Dodsland, the only place that was open that carried treats, and we would pile out of the car and scurry inside. Each of us would pick out one treat—I was partial to plain ripple chips; what can I say? I loved salt (still do). Once in a while we could purchase a pop from the hospital vending machine, but that was rare, so getting a vanload of groceries meant our fridge was full (along with our bellies). There were roasts or whole chickens cooking in the oven, potatoes boiling and gravy being mixed up with Dad's latest discovery: Bisto, a simple all-in-one gravy base! Mary introduced Dad's pallet to different things, then he would bring it home and teach us! It was a whole new adventure! I couldn't get on board with the sour cream, though, that just sounded wrong. Dad also enjoyed making a homemade soup with the lentils or peas he grew in the field. One of us would go to the grain bin and collect a few cups, he would let them soak overnight and then he would mix what seemed like every leftover we had into a pot and add the lentils or peas. It wasn't quite as bad as it sounds, but certainly not my favourite.

I don't know where Dad got the money to wine and dine Mary, and I didn't ask. Sometimes the phone, power or gas was cut off. He paid for hotel rooms and fine dining, but we had no phone.

Chapter 18

Forecast Looks Cloudy

I'm not exactly sure when it happened, but the dark, dank clouds of depression that had once hung over our family farm began casting shadows where there had once been light. The drinking, lack of food in the refrigerator and incessant arguing served as constant reminders of the depression which seeped back into my father's soul, tainting every relationship he had. Back then we didn't use terms like depression, but even without proper terminology, there was no denying the darkness. Like a familiar cloak, it enveloped him, confining him to his bedroom, taking comfort in the one cool friend that never left his side, a Molson Canadian beer.

Trips to Saskatoon became less frequent but ones to the bar increased. We were back to less food on our plates since the boys had both moved out. Kim and I no longer took lunches to school, but every once in a while we would sneak into Dad's bedroom and dig through the stash of pocket change he left in his rumpled, dirt-caked green Peavey Mart pants. We only needed a couple of dollars to buy chips or maybe a fresh pizza bun from the canteen at school. At home, we got by on crackers layered with margarine, toast with Cheez Whiz or peanut butter, and bologna. Social Services had been called when we were young kids, so I am surprised they weren't brought back in to do another home assessment when we were teenagers. Things were far worse than when we were young children.

Dad liked to say "No" a lot. If we wanted to go over to a friend's for a visit, he would say "No" without a reason; just a simple "No." This did not impress me. Being a stubborn and somewhat selfish seventeen-year-old, my social life was important, so we differed. The frustration was compounded when he would make note that Kim and I were girls and didn't need to go out. Perhaps it was from fear of how the world would treat us or the natural protection a father feels for his daughters, but it didn't feel that way. Staying at home enclosed by those familiar panel board brown walls which only became uglier over time was stifling. We were girls and wore that title with the shame we thought it evoked. I recall when my body started changing, I purposely wore larger sweaters and bulky layers so as not to share my budding womanhood. I didn't want to be noticed this way. Hiding became a well-ingrained pattern that would be hard to break as an adult.

We could go to our friends' houses if we strategically planned it. It was all about timing. When I had a friend at our house and their parents came to pick them up, I would ask permission in front of my friend. Dad didn't want to look like a complete jerk, but I sensed the seething just below the surface. It didn't faze me—I wanted what I wanted, and it didn't matter how it made him feel. His "Yes" was usually laced with disapproval, but to me it was a win.

Perhaps if I took some time away from my self-absorbed teenage brain, I would have noticed the simple yet significant changes happening within the walls of our towering old white farmhouse. Dad's marathon conversations on the phone with Mary were replaced with Kim or me stretching that new extra-long phone cord Dad had purchased at RadioShack through the kitchen and around the corner to the staircase where we would try to gain our privacy to call the friends we had just spent the previous six hours with at school. There was no nagging us to get off because he had no one to call. Since this was of great benefit to us, we didn't mind. We knew they had broken up but could not quite sort out why. It was the cloud that hung over the farm but mostly over Father's heart.

The thing about heartache is that it freezes into every crevice of your being, settling in like snow blankets the once rich and fertile soil. It freezes you in your tracks, and you can't move or get away from it. It's there in every corner. I could not ignore the sadness that sat inside my father's soul, so I would knock on his bedroom door and check to see if he was okay every once in a while, and I was usually met with resistance. He was working hard to build a wall between himself and his sorrows, and I was contemplating the best approach to break through. Instinctively, I sensed the placement of the bricks, the wall they created, the rigid edges of strained conversation or the loud cries of heartache hardening a heart once loved. I felt it all through him. We had been close when I was little, and I longed to find that sense of security again. I wanted to find that place within his heart where happiness dwelled and shine blissful light on it. Where this light would come from, well, I never planned that far ahead, and I suppose I knew I would never have to. That light belonged to Mary, and I was certain there was no replacement. She was a once in a lifetime kind of love for Dad, and no one could hold a candle to her.

Darkness and sadness took up residency inside the house, trickling slowly into everything and everyone. Like a slow rain, our hearts absorbed this sadness as our own. When you're living in the thick of darkness, it's difficult to determine what pain belongs to you and what pain is of other origins. Families that aren't necessarily close still sense the shift; we sensed changes and felt our way through both conversation and silence.

When Dad had been drinking, he would occasionally tell me pieces of what happened. Mary wanted to get married, and Dad couldn't offer her that. They had parted ways mutually, or so the story went, but I knew that wasn't the case because it was clearly not what he wanted. He genuinely wanted to marry her, too, but his situation presented too many obstacles, the most serious being that he was already married. He couldn't see a way through the thick fog of uncertainty. He couldn't figure out how to trust the universe or God enough to make that leap and know it would be okay. For him there was too much at stake, too many unknowns. Little did he know this single decision would alter his entire future. I oscillated between feeling sorry for him and feeling an unhealthy rebellion brew in the pit of my soul. Both places left me unsettled.

Chapter 19

Silence Broken

Attending school in rural Saskatchewan, just like in every other small town, means your friends are often due to geography rather than common interests. Social status adds another layer and is usually inherited. Chances are everyone's parents went to school together, and if they were "cool," you might be, too, which seems to still be part of the small-town culture nowadays.

Even though my family had been there many years, as many as most of the farming families in the community, fitting in socially to the popular crowd eluded me given my dad's alcoholism. The spotlight was on us, but not in the way I wanted. Sometimes it would phase me, but for the most part I worked hard at being a friend to the ones I had. Kim and I tended to share friends, which is also a cultural norm of small towns. Grades above and below all intermix and mingle.

One thing that set us apart from some of the other students was the way we were raised. Even though no one said it to our faces, we felt it. Being raised by our father created a stigma. Single parent households were not common in our tightly-knit community, so we stuck out.

Eventually, Dad's drinking pushed me to my breaking point. There was no reasoning with him. His mood was dark, and the parameters he placed on Kimberley and me had become difficult to navigate, especially since we wanted a social life and maybe even boyfriends. With both my brothers moving out, Kim and I were left to fend for ourselves.

Dad wouldn't allow Kim to go for her driver's test, which meant we were stuck without rides to get the necessities, such as food. When I turned sixteen, he wouldn't let me go either, but instead of cowering to my father, I called Uncle Perry, Mom's youngest brother. We were pretty close with all our mother's siblings, and we depended on a few of them to help us get through the hard times.

"Uncle Perry? Hi, it's Diana."

"Diana? What do you want?" Uncle Perry said in the typical sarcastic voice he used where I was unsure if he was being funny or serious.

Hearing the joking in his voice, I relaxed.

"Kim and I and our friend Tanya all need our driver's licenses. Right now, Kim and I can't even go to town to get food—we are stuck here. We can't visit friends or anything. Do you think you could maybe take us to get our license?"

The question fell out of me sooner than I would have liked. I wanted to build up to this conversation, but that wasn't the case.

"You want me to take three teenagers to Kindersley for their license on the same day? Do you think I'm crazy?"

I was back to being unsure if he was kidding with me or going to string me along and make me squirm a bit.

"What did your dad say about this?"

"Well, to be honest, I haven't asked yet. I figured I might just want to beg for forgiveness instead of asking for permission since his favourite word in the English dictionary is 'No.'"

Well, Uncle Perry ended up taking us to Kindersley to give that old driver's license a kick at the can. When Aaron was home on weekends from university, he helped us practice. It took a couple of tries. After Kim and I failed the first time, Dad was all aboard the "I told you so" train with a stop at "You can't do it" station, so I had to dig deep inside and learn to keep his lack of belief in me—his opinion of me—at bay. If I couldn't do that, I would never leave the farm. Freedom was on the line and I knew it.

We eventually passed, and freedom was ours if Dad would have ever let use the car! Parents not wanting to lend their kids a car may be common because it's too hard on their conscience to let them out of the house without their protection, but it wasn't that way with us. Kim and I needed our license for more than going out; we needed it to live! Food supply was always short because Dad only brought home the bare necessities.

The breaking point happened on a hot summer day when Dad was totally inebriated. Arguments were commonplace, but some were worse than others. I had a sharp tongue, which was problematic at times for us both. We argued about a boy, and the temper I hadn't learned to harness (like Kim had) heated to the point of boiling. Dad had initially given me permission to spend the weekend at a boy's house, but after consulting with Mary—they were at an on-again, off-again phase of their relationship (mostly off, but Dad tended to reach out for advice and to soothe his loneliness)—he retracted permission. It's a hard pill to swallow when someone else who does not live with you and really only hears one side of the story tries to parent you. Plus, I didn't take kindly to the idea of him changing his mind last-minute. My boyfriend lived about an hour away, had a nice family my dad had met, and I had done nothing to risk his disapproval. Well, perhaps the back talk wasn't always necessary, but, as I said, I had a sharp tongue and an equal wit.

This argument took a path none had ever taken before, but I felt it necessary to call him out on his bullshit. Before I could catch myself, three words hit the air in a rage: "You're an ALCOHOLIC!" As soon as my mind caught my tongue, I realized the magnitude of what I had just spoken. He stood there, stunned. Fearing the wrath that would ensue, I quickly darted out the patio doors, running as fast as my scrawny legs would carry me. I end up behind the Quonset with my dog by my side. The air was hot and sticky, and I felt Rex nudge up beside me as my tears streamed. I was spent, but I had to remember to slow down and breath because I couldn't afford to have an asthma attack at a time like this! I didn't know if Dad would take me to the hospital, and even if he did, I wouldn't want the people there to smell the stench of alcohol on his breath. I gained my composure and pet the dog with my right hand while wiping my eyes with my left.

As I brought my face to meet the sky, I heard footsteps and my sister rounded the corner. Kim wasn't one to get involved in family disputes—she was a keep-it-to-yourself kind of girl—so this was an odd occurrence. As she approached, my eyes focused on hers. She was serious but not angry. Suddenly, the cool and inapproachable teenage girl I had come to know did something unpredictable. Sliding down the warm steel Quonset door, she planted herself beside me as if hunkering down to watch the summer clouds pass by just like we used to. She chose to comfort me, and she wrapped her slender arms around my shaky frame and whispered words of reassurance that echoed in my heart days later. This was a complete role reversal. Being the talker of the two, and certainly more outgoing than Kim, I often found myself in the front of any line, person, battle, confrontation or discussion defending Kim or myself if need be. Kim spoke so little to others that I'd always felt compelled to do it for both of us, but this time Kim was my big sister and I the vulnerable little one. The warmth I felt was not just from the blistering heat but from the opening of a vault long held tightly closed.

The words finally hit the air, and the silence lifted along with the pretending. We never talked about the drinking. It wasn't only Dad's dirty little secret, it was ours, and that day I found the courage to say what everyone else had been thinking for years. That day changed the course of our family forever.

As I sneaked back into the house, I caught a glimpse of him passed out on the couch. I cried a lot that night. It was a huge release of emotions that had been in there since I was a little girl hearing him throwing up for the first time. The trauma of what he had done to our family was just starting to trickle into my stream, and I realized the alcohol had become like cancer in our house. It was the reason

Chris didn't come home anymore, the reason behind so many heated debates with all of us kids, and the reason why we felt no stability in our lives. The alcohol robbed us of our only dependable parent. We had done our best to parent ourselves and navigate life, and it would only get worse.

Chapter 20

Shackles and Freedom

Leaving home felt like an event that was forever in the future, something that would never come to fruition. I logged many hours laying on my plush pink comforter thinking of my future, stuffed animals still assembled in the left corner symbolizing the irony of my thoughts; a child breaking through to adulthood. But was I really ever a child? The idea of putting myself out into the world was a longing for a simple, quiet freedom. Freedom was the only plan I ever had.

I had not given much thought to what I wanted to "be" when I grew up, even though everyone seems to ask that question of every teenager who was finishing high school. Other than a singer or a writer, I had no plans for a career or the future. Auntie Betty said I should go to school to be a secretary. The idea didn't thrill me, but I wanted to get out of that place and I needed an education, so I applied to community college in Saskatoon. It wasn't my dream but a way to save myself.

When you meet life in survival mode day in and day out you don't allow yourself the luxury of planning, so I relied on my aunt to help me figure out my next steps. The daydream hours were spent thinking of having my own space—an apartment!—and the freedom to buy some of the things I had wanted for a long time. I could go out with friends whenever I pleased and, probably most significantly,

I would finally have a fridge full of food. I would pay for all of this with my student loans, and Aaron helped me fill out the applications.

It was a glorious and painful reality knowing I was a far cry from fitting the mould of the limited belief system my dad had for most women, but especially his daughters. I was to find a rich man, marry and start a family. I never thought that one day I may become a mother. I already was parenting myself and had been making meals for an entire family for years, so why would I want to parent someone else? I felt independent going to college and also somewhat of a disappointment as he had never planned for this. It went without saying that I would foot the entire bill myself.

As my boyfriend Dave and I loaded up my childhood in the box of his dad's Chevy pickup truck, my dad slowly walked to the shop. I motioned to Dave that I was going to say goodbye to my father and walked towards the shop. I slowly opened the door, letting the bright late summer light wash over the dim lights of the shop. I faintly saw the image of a man, my father, crouched by the air compressor, fiddling with an air socket. This was a sight I had seen a thousand times over, but the air was different this time. The winds of change were blowing through and taking my dad's baby girl with them.

Our conversation was awkward and forced, neither of us sure which words to use to meet our emotions. He asked the standard questions, making sure I had everything I needed, asking what day I started classes and wishing me luck with the public transit system of Saskatoon. He seemed happy Dave and my friends would help me move into the apartment, but he never once offered to come in and help. Looking back now, my self-sufficiency may have come off as lack of needing him. Needing parents wasn't necessary in my world. Daydreams of having a heartwarming childhood played like a film in my mind, but, like that film, it was always outside myself. I planned my move to freedom seamlessly, and those plans did not include him.

Meeting my dad's eyes that late August afternoon, I saw something I had become accustomed to: sadness. There was a distinct difference though. The sadness wasn't the familiar one about his weary heart or troubled finances. No. It felt more like knowing I would never live at that farm again. I would never again be confined by those walls, shackled or bound by what I deemed oppressive and outdated hierarchy and rules. He would wake in the same house he had for the previous fifty-one years, but tomorrow would be different. His contentious daughter would be taking on the world two hours away while he battled the same struggles. As confined as I felt in that farmhouse, it bound him even more so. The towering farmhouse kept his personal struggles a secret, or so he liked to believe.

Our hug was unusual. Affection was not something we shared as a family, so when my dad reached gracelessly towards me, my feet stepped me back. I moved uneasily forward, catching the hurt he felt and wrapping it tightly in my arms. We hugged, tight and strong. As unfamiliar as it was, there was a comfort; the first real father/daughter moment we had shared in years.

I left him in his shop to tinker on the combine. Harvest was in full swing, and repairs on the old red Massy seemed endless. In my selfish teenage way, I drove out of that yard sensing freedom and giving no further thought to the moment we shared and what it meant to him.

Chapter 21

Directionless

Living in Saskatoon was pretty great initially. Dave and I could spend as much time as we wanted together, I made friends quickly at college, and I found the public transit system relatively easy to figure out. I got my bus pass at City Hall, right across from the downtown bus terminal and less than a block from my school. I took in my surroundings enough to navigate my way around downtown on foot, and one such place was the mall! My student loan money had come in at the start of September, so after I paid for my tuition and books I took myself to the mall for some new brand-name clothes. Many of my clothes were hand-me-downs from my cousin Emma and her cousin Jackie. They had good taste and the clothes were usually pretty nice. I rarely got anything new more than once a year, usually at the start of school. No way was I going to buy cheap Zellers jean jackets and T-shirts. I wanted what all my friends had. Also, for the first time in my life I bought myself some bras that fit! As strange as that sounds, I had not had a proper bra, ever. I wore my mom's old ones as we had not gone shopping since Grade 7 when Kim and I went with Dad and Mary. A lot had changed since then, but somehow we just made do. Gravity was kind, except for during gym class.

I found the Club Monaco store and bought myself one of those sweaters that everyone else had already worn for a good year. Next, I found myself in La Senza buying a few bras and some panties. Then

I went to another store to get some brand-name jeans! I found a cute dress and some fancy shoes at Le Château which I spent far too much on, but it felt great to spoil myself.

Next, some friends and I drove to Walmart where I got bath towels! There was a total of four bath towels in our house, and they were from our parents' wedding in 1971. It was 1996, so those towels had dried our skin for twenty-five years and looked worse for wear! I found a cute shower curtain which had a matching bath-mat and waste basket, and I just had to have them! As a graduation present, my dad bought me a queen-size comforter with a floral design which went perfectly in my bedroom. I brought my bed from home, never really thinking about what I would sleep on when I went home to visit. The bed had no frame and sat on the floor just as it had in the farmhouse. I needed to purchase a mirror and some plastic free-standing drawers. I had never given much thought to my "dresser" until going to my friends' houses where they had chests of drawers! I had more of an old school desk. I bought some hangers, organized my closet and decided my dresser would now serve as a desk. I carefully placed the percaline kitty Lisa had bought me along with some knick-knacks and a green lamp Aaron had given to me. The rest of the house was furnished with garage sale items and old furniture from my friend Tanya's parents.

I capped off my shopping with some groceries at Superstore, a wonderous place I had never been to. There was never much to eat at home, so I made sure my cupboards and fridge were full. I never wanted that feeling of my body eating itself in an attempt to find some sustenance again. At eighteen years of age, I had finally reached one hundred pounds and stretched up to five feet, two inches tall, the shortest of the four kids.

In the big city I enjoyed things like takeout, wing nights with friends and cooking for others. Much of my time was spent with David and his roommate Marlon. Marlon's parents owned a small-town grocery store, so we always had an abundance of food to cook. I spent weekends with David and his friends and family, and I had all but abandoned mine. As much as I am ashamed to admit this, I wanted little to do with my hometown. I kept in contact with a few of my friends, but we had disbursed around various cities and provinces for college and, unlike teenagers today, contacting them meant calling, which meant a phone bill I had to pay.

Plenty symbolized every possible way I could be rejected. I know it sounds dramatic, but it was rational to my eighteen-year-old self. My family had been on display, as I suppose all small-town families are when things aren't picture perfect. I longed to meld somewhere, to be accepted, to be good enough. As much as I felt I didn't fit into my community, I felt I didn't fit into my family even more so. Deep shame trickled into my veins, and I made friends with it. I understood it and soon found myself listening to all the ways I wasn't good enough and believing them. It felt suffocating and produced a desperate need to run inside me. Leaving home was the first time I ever had a sense of anonymity and the ability to recreate myself. I thought judgements trapped my growth, but little did I know the judgements weren't coming from the outside. The harshest judgements I was facing were from my own thoughts.

All I felt I was known for in Plenty was my "dysfunctional" family, and I wanted to run from that "Les Kirk's daughter" label. I ran away from anything that reminded me of alcoholism and illness. Plenty knew all my secrets, and the urge to run away bore into my soul. Interestingly, as I reflect now, perhaps my dad and I really weren't that different. Maybe we were both following our urge to run; him by drinking endless Molson Canadians inside the safe confines of his acres of land and me straight into life without a plan.

In March of the following year, David and I had been having some problems. I had moved in January and felt rather comfortable with a roommate in a safer part of the city. I was needy and clingy, none of which I wanted to admit. I depended on him for everything from going grocery shopping to spending weekends together when he was back from his truck driving job which took him on the road most of the time. He had asked me to move in together before January. As much as I was not ready for this, I knew in my soul that if I did that, my dad would all but disown me! Even two hours apart, the fear of my dad's wrath seared scars on my heart that never fully healed. Each one of them oozed painfully at the thought of David and I living together. I told him no, but part of me wanted to say yes. I was an adult on my own but not acting very adult-like. I allowed my father's opinions to dictate what I did, and I sought David's approval to the point where it was suffocating us both. When he started going out with the boys more and ignoring me, instead of coolly and calmly walking away, I clung on as tight as I could. He eventually slipped out of my reach.

Something inside of me needed this relationship, not so much for love but for security. What I truly wanted was his family. When I met David a few years before, I had not felt attraction. He seemed nice enough, and my friend said he liked me, so I gave it a shot. When we started dating and I met his family, I was instantly in love! His parents were wonderful, solid people with strong values, work ethic and a moral compass. They were the family that got up early on Sunday to attend church and sat around the table at meals updating each other on the happenings of the day. They were the family that drove their kids to Ukrainian dance competitions and hockey. There were four kids, like my family, but more spread out in age. They were a busy family, the family I ever longed to be a part of.

Chapter 22

Seeking Help

It was a rainy Wednesday evening when I gingerly stepped down the damp staircase that was lit only by the glistening streetlight. The rain danced with the wind, blowing heavy drops against my face. As I made my way to the basement door, I took a deep breath, unsure of what waited behind. The instructions I received on the other end of the phone was that the meeting would take place at 8:00 p.m. in the basement of the United Church on 11th Street. I stood there and reconsidered the decision as fear crept in. But it was accompanied by something else: a feeling I could not shake. Perhaps it was curiosity? Whatever it was, it always pushed me forward.

The meeting was underway, and it stopped abruptly when I entered. Was I in the right place?

"Is this the Al-Anon meeting?" I asked awkwardly.

It was. The women ushered me into their circle and one lady grabbed a chair that had been against the wall. Something didn't feel quite right, but I quietly sat down, gesturing a thank you for the chair and apologies for interrupting.

I shared my name and age with the group but nothing further. When asked if I wished to share why I was there, I politely declined, trying to quiet the feeling of unease settling inside me. Something was wrong there. I was not among the right age demographic, but my curiosity kept me in my seat.

Listening intently I verified what I already knew: I was in the wrong group. The women were sharing stories of living with an alcoholic, and I could relate to that part, but the people they lived with were their spouses not their parents, so I raised my hand to ask a question.

"Hi, my name is Diana. I am the daughter of an alcoholic," I say quietly.

"Hi Diana, I'm Lillian. How old are you, Sweetie?" asked a pleasant looking middle-aged lady with blue rimmed glasses as she peeked past her bifocals to get a better look at me.

"I'm nineteen. I want to come to a meeting with other kids of alcoholics. I need help coping with my dad's drinking."

I sucked the air in tight to my lungs to keep my composure.

"That's tough for sure, but I believe you are too old for the youth program, Sugar. Looks like you're stuck here with all of us old hens!"

Everyone in the room chuckled, but I was more uncomfortable. My face, pained, forced more of an explanation from the others. They felt terrible that I could no longer be with the children but assured me I was welcome to sit with them. They validated the fact that I was a young woman, an adult, but I couldn't have felt further from being a grown-up at that moment. For the first time in my life, I was reaching out to speak with others and heal together with other children of alcoholics.

Sinking back into my chair, I quieted my voice and wrestled with the concept I had just been told. *Since I am nineteen I cannot be with other kids that may understand my plight, what I went through, how I felt?* I was stuck there listening to women talk about their drunk husbands. I didn't understand on any level how that made sense. I was the child of an alcoholic, and turning nineteen didn't change the fact that I was still my father's child, was raised in an alcoholic environment and wanted to speak with other kids who had faced the same choices as I did. I could not relate to those women, and the concept as to why they stayed was something I could not get my young brain around. I saw these women and felt they had the right to stand up and leave their drunk husbands. My foolish teenage mind didn't understand why someone would choose to stay with an alcoholic. I did not see reasons like they had no money or had endured years of emotional or physical abuse. Perhaps they had no education or maybe they had children to think of and needed to secure plans for their safety and their children's. No, none of those rational thoughts popped into my mind. Instead, I was dumbfounded by the fact that I had been placed with a group of middle-aged women who were married to alcoholics, most old enough to be my mother.

I listened to stories of what their husbands had done this week for over an hour. Pretty much ruined their lives. Each woman supported the others through a soft squeeze of the hand, pat on the leg or comforting words of encouragement. I sat in silence, curious about the thought that I could leave but didn't. I didn't fit, but there was an odd comfort in not fitting in—a knowledge that I have never fit anywhere.

At the end of the evening, we all replaced our chair in their resting spots, stacking one atop the other against the wall. A couple of women came up to me, grabbed my hands, patted them and thanked me for coming. I smiled cordially and ducked out the same way I came in. It was still raining as I walked back to my basement suite. I didn't pull my hood up to shield my hair from the rain. Instead, I let the drops blend with my tears as my heart sank in disappointment. I had high hopes for that meeting. It was my step towards healing, but instead I was left deflated.

That night I turned to the only place I have ever felt right: alone in a dimly-lit bedroom with my thoughts, a pen and some paper. It was there where my judgements and decompressions took place. It was there where I hung my heart and felt no rejection. It was there where I unearthed the pains of my soul.

With the understanding that I would not be allowed in the children's age group of Al-Anon, I decided not to attend another meeting. This disappointment appeared on the papers that were soaked in my tears.

Chapter 23

The Choices We Make

I have contemplated this decision for the last twenty-two years. Within the contemplation, I sat with another decision: to share it here, with you, releasing it with the possibility of facing a life sentence from some. I could also let it quietly continue to rest inside my heart, safe from critical words and sharp looks of judgement. What comes to mind, however, is a well-known quote by Maya Angelou: "Do the best until you know better. Then when you know better, do better." With that, I have come to the conclusion that perhaps someone will heal from my honesty. Perhaps that someone is me.

The room was cold and blurred. I had just turned nineteen and was still full of youthful arrogance accompanied with the desperate need to please. It was uncomfortable to be in my skin that day. I looked at the blank walls of the hospital unable to make out objects, let alone the shape of them. I didn't realize I couldn't wear my contacts because I couldn't be put under while wearing them. See, that right there is a good example of the youthful arrogance. My glasses were in my apartment not that far away, but I had no one to get them. That day, as many other days of life, I faced the world blindly. Lately, events had melded together, and it was difficult to pull apart and decipher what was real and what was not. God, I wish that day was not real.

As I walked the hallway to the surgery room, I hung my head in shame. Other than the nurses, I was alone, but I took no comfort or solace in it. I wanted Dave there, but he dropped me off. When we initially met with the nurses, they told him I will would be able to go home in roughly eight hours, so he said he would be back then to pick me up. It's like he delivered me to a shift at work, his casual goodbye betraying the gravity of the day. He kept any feelings of fear, regret or upset to himself, so I walked that march of death alone. Blind. Terrified.

I walked into the room and am met with bright lights and people wearing gowns. The doctor greeted me, and I reluctantly shook his hand, thinking, *This is no reason to shake hands.* My body trembled as I climbed onto the surgery table and laid down.

"Diana Kirk, nineteen years old, six weeks pregnant, is here today for an abortion," he said.

The words, full of horror, stung my heart, signalling the tears that had sat just below my lids for the past hour. Shame didn't feel like a strong enough word to hold this secret that everyone in this room now knows, so it trickled down my cheeks.

I closed my eyes and try to keep out reality. I did not want this, but I had no choice. I could not stand up for myself, which was a running theme in my life. I was so afraid Dave would leave if I didn't go through with it. Suddenly I felt a soft hand, and a nurse gingerly wiped my hair from my forehead, smiling while another tied my left arm to a foam-covered plank sticking out from the side of the table. She wanted to start the IV, but I was shaking in fear. I was cold and in shock. The other nurse grabbed a warmed blanket and immediately covered me. She brought her head close to my face and smiled, her bright, sky blue eyes looking at me with sincere caring. Eyes don't tell lies, and she knew I was afraid. While stroking my hair, she smiled. Nothing could be said to make what was about to happen better, she knew that, so all she could give me was the presence of her being, her compassion, her understanding, and absolutely no judgement. I felt it all through her touch and in her eyes. Tears pooled in the corners of my green eyes; I was so afraid. She wiped them away and leaned close to my ear.

"I am here, Sweetie. I won't leave. I got you."

The anesthesiologist appeared above my head, mask in hand, ready to quiet my world. Once again, the nurse's face met mine.

"Are you ready, Sweetie?" she said. "I'll be right here."

I gave a quick nod, counted backwards from ten, and sometime before I got to one, I was out.

Waking up alone in recovery, I was told things went "well." For me that meant I successfully killed a baby. The baby Dave and I created. This was not a success, it was a damn nightmare! The baby was gone, but the sick pit in my stomach had grown. I needed to get out of there.

I was wheeled back to my room where my clothes awaited my return, tucked away in a locker, the key in David's pocket. He was sitting in the corner chair. I couldn't make out his expression as the nurse reiterated that everything went well. My heart continued to sink.

Once she left the room, Dave unlocked my possessions from the locker, and I put in my contacts and got dressed. I was not ready to talk, to face this world. I just wanted to go home and cry. Dave said a couple of our friends wanted to go out with us, but I was uninterested. If he wanted to, he can. I needed to be alone and take time to process what I had just done.

The drive back to the apartment was silent. I wanted to tell him how angry I was that this happened, how much I did not want to have an abortion and how much I hurt. But I cannot. I cannot find my voice. It was locked somewhere in my heart. Or maybe it was taken away with our baby. I looked at him, deep pain spread across my face as he asked if I was okay. I wasn't, and for the first time I saw his hurt.

That night we laid in bed holding each other, and I cried myself to sleep. Sometimes I still do that, twenty-three years later.

Chapter 24

The Year Of Change

Nineteen ninety nine was a year where I started making decisions for me. Well, not initially. In December of 1998, I had given up my apartment where I lived with a couple friends. On January 1, 1999, I moved to Dave's hometown of Cudworth, Saskatchewan, about forty-five minutes northeast of Saskatoon, with two other friends. Somehow, I was back to a small town. I loved his family and being in Cudworth meant I would be able to see them more. Sadly, I could not get my typing speed to sixty words per minute to complete my secretarial school, and once I had the abortion, I didn't want to show my face in that school again. I had told one of my friends what had happened and she tried to reach out, but my shame pushed her away.

Life with Dave was hit and miss. He seemed to only make time for me when it worked for him. After the abortion, I experienced a level of grief that I couldn't share with anyone. I wore a thick cloak of shame and guilt that felt so heavy it embedded the pain in my soul. I could not bear to speak. The only person that shared this burden didn't seem to care too much about how I felt, so I kept quiet for the sake of keeping Dave happy.

I could be a needy girlfriend—calling all the time, wanting to make plans—and I sensed this annoyed Dave, perhaps even suffocated him. When I moved in with Tanya and Craig, it was

Dave who strongly encouraged it. I didn't know if I should at first but looking back now I see why. He had plans to break it off for a while, and even though he didn't want to be with me, he knew I didn't have much family support, so living with Tanya and Craig could fill some of that void.

I wasn't living out in Cudworth long before Dave broke it off at a party. A couple weekends before while we were drinking with friends, someone said to Dave, "But you love Diana!"

"No he doesn't," I drunkenly blurted. "He told me a while ago he doesn't love me."

Things got really quiet around the card table. I was standing at the staircase facing the dining room table. Everyone was looking at me, including Dave.

"He didn't mean it, who wouldn't love you!" Tanya said, trying to make light of the situation.

I smugly remarked, "Ask him yourself."

Dave, turned red now, burned with embarrassment, and we went upstairs to have yet another fight. It was really too bad I didn't have the self-worth or courage to break it off with him right then and there. I had to keep holding on. For what, I am unsure.

A couple of weeks later, Dave sat me down in my bedroom and told me we should end this. I was a mess all night after he left. People paraded in and out of my room feeding me drinks because I didn't want to go downstairs. When I finally decided to make an appearance, he had decided there was nothing else going on in town so he should come back to the party. I walked towards the staircase in my drunken stupor and fell right down the twelve stairs. People rushed to help me up, but I bounced back up right away, unphased by the physical pain yet deeply aware of the emotional. Dave was the first one to try to help me, but several guys removed him from the party. A few good friends took me back upstairs and we continued the in and out visits until I passed out.

The next day, Tanya, Craig and I cleaned up from the party. I was noticeably quiet, partly due to the hangover, mostly due to the heartache. Tanya and Craig had a Sunday supper at his parents' house in Saskatoon, and she fretted over the idea of leaving me alone with my thoughts, which was sweet, but I needed to be alone. I nestled myself into a comfy chair by the window. The only lights brightening the house were from the streetlights. Pulling a blanket around me, I curled my legs underneath and watched the snow gently fall. Everywhere was quiet; the house, the street, my heart.

Funny, did you know that tears can fall as silently as the snow? I played the previous few years back in my mind, grabbing more tissue to soak up the remnants of my broken heart. There was a deep, profound knowing that this had to happen, so I was not angry. But wasn't relieved either. Instead, I sat somewhere between numb and scared. I was nineteen, unemployed, had no money and will never move back home. I felt directionless, like I'd let myself down. Since high school I'd wrapped my life around a boy. I embedded myself in his loving family, allowing his parents to envelop me and shower me with love and support. I loved spending time with his siblings too. Christmas, Easter, church and any other family event felt nice, felt normal. Instead of being gazed upon with pity or judgment in public, I blended in with this beautiful family that was respected by the community. My story in this town wasn't visible, and for the first time I realized that was what I would truly miss. Dave's family was not mine. His parents would always be his.

A tidal wave of grief hit me. I was overwhelmed with the thoughts of what I had left, which felt like very little. I had to figure out what to do, but the thoughts of moving on cascaded over my mind and left me with a sick feeling in my stomach. Eventually my tears put me to sleep as I curled up, knees to chest, blanket tucked tightly around my feeble frame. Exhaustion had set in, and as much as my mind wanted to continue to race, my body won this battle.

In the morning, I awoke exhausted and with a sore body. I hadn't moved all night. I arched my back and put my legs down onto the cool floor. A thought came to me: it was time to tell my dad. Since dating Dave and adopting his family as my own, I had continued to pull away from my core family unit. But now there was the stark realization that this was what my support looked like. I dialled the phone which was mounted along the staircase wall and was surprised when Dad answered. He hated answering calls, especially during the week as it is more than likely a bill collector. My palms were sweaty as I recounted the events of the previous few days. He exploded in anger. Unsure of what I did to anger him, I tirelessly defended myself to the point that the conversation wasn't even making sense. He threw in comments like, "I never liked Dave. He grabbed your leg at the Garth Brooks concert when we went, and I didn't like that. But he comes from money, and you could have had it made with that family! What did I tell you? Marry rich!" After that rant was over, he moved on to the harsh judgements about me not finishing school, that he had no money to support me so don't even ask, and that I can move back home if I want. Yeah, this conversation really made me want to move back to that train wreck. Coping with stress for my dad consisted of slurs, judgements and reminders of how I was a disappointment. He mocked the fact that in secretary school I could not get my typing speed fast enough so I didn't graduate. If he only knew that when I was supposed to be finishing school, I was going through one of the darkest times in my life, maybe he would ease up. He reminded that I had a student loan that he will not pay a dime for, yet another reminder that he cannot "afford" me. Normally I would defend myself, but the break-up took the fire out of me. I had nothing left to give, so I just allowed him to hurl the insults and demons at me. Part of my mind knew they weren't true, but the other part felt they were exactly what I deserved for abandoning him.

Near the end of our conversation my dad asked me what my plan was, and, embarrassingly, I did not have an answer. Again, the invitation to come home stood. I could not do it; I knew in my bones. I may not have been strong, I may have been unemployed and had no money or self-worth, but by God I would not move home!

Tanya and Craig were at work as I headed back upstairs to battle the demons that Dad reminded me of. *What am I going to do?* It was mid-March and no jobs had been posted in the area. I had no vehicle, so I couldn't drive to Wakaw, a nearby town, for work. I was limited in this small community of eight hundred people. As I contemplated my bleak future, I was startled by a knock at the door. Confused as to who it could be, I gingerly made my way down the carpeted steps and peeked out the living room window to see if I recognized the vehicle. It was Dave's parents' van.

I opened the door, and Ruth walked in and gave me a great big hug. I looked like death warmed over and hadn't gotten out of my pajamas all day, but embracing Ruth felt like a hug from the mother I always wished was mine. Tears brimmed at the thought of knowing everything had changed. She never was and would never be my mother. Still, the warmth from her embrace somehow settled the sick feeling I'd had in my stomach since talking with my dad earlier.

She sat at the kitchen table as I grabbed us some cold water. When I met her gaze, I saw the same love she had shared with me since we met. There was something special about Ruth. She possessed a genuine kindness that is rare in this world. *I am going to miss being a part of your family*, I thought to myself. Ruth broke our silence with that warm smile I adored.

"Diana, I am so sorry you are going through this," she said. "Dave, Jack and I had a long talk the other night after you two broke up. He does not see what a beautiful person you are. He just isn't ready for someone as mature and strong as you."

Her words echoed in my head. Mature? Strong? The look of confusion on my face alerted her to elaborate.

"You have been through a lot, Diana. You have not had it easy. I know it seems like a confusing and stressful time for you, but I know you, you will make it through this. I also need you to know that when we spoke with David we asked if we could still be a part of your life if he was OK with that. He said yes and told us that he knows you will need us. So I am here to tell you that you have our support."

The powerful relief that overcame me during this tender moment exploded from me and I leapt up from my chair and bounced over to Ruth who was already up from her chair, arms wide and ready to receive my battered mind. Her embrace reassured my soul in a way I hadn't felt in days. Tears streamed down my cheeks, soaking Ruth's red sweater, so I pulled back and went searching for a tissue. I was still in awe that I could still count on Ruth and Jack to be in my corner when Ruth sat back down and told me I needed a plan.

"What are you thinking you will do now? I would love to have you stay close by, but there really are no jobs," Ruth said with compassion and her wry little smile.

I nodded, but before I got a chance to respond, I knew she had already thought of an answer. Never were she or Jack disrespectful about my childhood or where I'd come from, but they also knew how strained my relationship was with my dad. We all knew I couldn't move back home because I may not make it out again.

"Have you talked with your Auntie Betty in Lloydminster?"

I knew where Ruth was going. I had not. Carrying around the shame of this break-up left my brain in a fog, so problem-solving had not be at the forefront of mind. Surviving had been my style my whole life, planning not so much.

"No, she doesn't know. I haven't called her. I'm not sure she if she is back from the States yet," I stammered.

Her and Uncle went to Nevada every winter and usually came back in March. Before I started dating Dave in 1995, I debated moving to Lloyd to go to college there. It would have been nice to have been close to my aunt and uncle, but once Dave came along that all changed. I followed a boy and not what I really wanted. My whole life to that point had been following the path others laid before me.

Ruth and I came to the same obvious conclusion: move in with Auntie Betty and Uncle Walt. It hit me like a brick. My aunt had told me a couple months before that I could move in with her, but I was still hopeful for some sort of relationship with Dave; I was not ready to see the writing on the wall. This time, however, I could decide where I wanted to go. I knew the winds were pushing me to the west, a farm south of Lloydminster, Alberta, the only place I really felt the love of a true home besides at Dave's. For the previous three years I had tried to make myself family to them, so it was a difficult realization to remember that I was not, nor would I ever be. I thought I satisfied this deep longing to find a family when I met him, but I had to keep searching instead.

After Tanya, Craig and I had supper that evening, I made the call that would change the trajectory of my life. Auntie answered on the third ring, her voice as loving and happy as it always was when I called. I pictured my mom's oldest sister, who looked quite a bit like my mom, and excitement and anxiety flowed through my body. Asking for what I need has always been a difficult thing for me. It demands that I state my needs and, as you've read throughout this book, I felt my needs weren't a priority for anyone, including me.

I started the conversation casually, asking about the weather, and then we moved on to my birthday coming up on March 21. She went on and on about how I was just this cute little baby with lots of hair! We giggled, and it eased my mind about the reason I called.

My voice shook somewhat as I said, "Auntie, can I ask you something?"

"Of course, Diana, what is it?"

There was no concern in her voice, just confident reassurance.

"Do you think I could maybe live with you guys for a while, please? I think it would be good for me. Dave and I broke up, and I need a fresh start."

Auntie paused for a minute and said, "I don't see why not, but I will have to ask Uncle first, OK?"

She agreed to call me back once she had an answer, but I already knew I would be moving in with them; my gut told me so. Sure enough, she called back shortly and said that after we got off the phone, my cousin Kevin, who had heard part of the conversation, said, "Mom, let her come live with us." I guess he knew it was right too.

Two weeks later was my twentieth birthday, so Tanya and Craig hosted a big shaker for me in celebration of my birthday and my impending move. Dave showed up, and I was feeling far more confident around him now that I had a plan. A couple of my friends were sad I was moving and tried to convince me to stay, but my friend Lindsay did the exact opposite. She pulled me into the bathroom and told me that this was my chance to make a better life for myself so I had better take it. At first it hurt my feelings, but one look in her eyes made me understand that this was coming from a place of love, of growth, of wanting me to succeed. She knew this was my only way to do that. And she was right.

That Monday, my aunt and uncle came to take me to their home. We loaded up their Ford truck with my meager belongings and set out on the icy pavement to their farm, to the place I knew would help heal the lost little girl I was and the floundering grown woman I had become.

Chapter 25

Time to Grow Up

I placed my belongings in an old antique dresser that had been tucked up against the wall in "the cave" bedroom, the most coveted bedroom every teenager in the house wanted. Their youngest son, Jay, had slept in it in for many years, and now it was passed down to me! As the baby of the family, I always brought up the tail end, so I rarely got privileges like that. It was nice and dark, a perfect setting for a perfect sleep.

As I arranged my clothes, I sat at the antique dresser/makeup station (it has a stool and mirror—probably more like a desk, but it is a beautiful piece for a dresser) and was overcome with a sense of relief. I didn't know what I would do for a job or a vehicle, but moving felt like the first right decision I'd made in many years.

I took the first couple of weeks to get my feet under me, with Auntie's help. She and I did some spring cleaning and talked about all kinds of things. Her home was big and beautiful, full of love. I think that's what made it so beautiful to me. Since I had no money, helping her clean was a way I could earn my keep, which also felt good.

I called home when I was still at Tanya's to tell my dad of my new plan. I was met with anger, of course, but this time I found my fight, my voice. I knew I would need a car because I was twenty minutes from Lloydminster, so driving to work would be my only option. Dad happened to have an old Oldsmobile that was so full of rust on the driver's side that if you washed it the interior was likely to get wet, so I thought I would ask him for it. He was enraged by the request for some reason, but I knew if I could just make him understand that moving in with Betty and Walt wasn't personal, it was about better work opportunities in Lloydminster, perhaps he would see the logic. Somehow, I managed to be right.

My aunt drove me down to Plenty to pick it up once I landed a job at a local clothing store in Lloydminster. My dad was not the type of man who gave stuff away (especially to me), so I knew this was a big deal. My aunt did a great job building him up and thanking him for helping me. She said we were all a team that wanted me to succeed. She was right, I am sure Dad did want to see me succeed, but his anger about me not moving home clouded it. I felt like he held no pride in me, so I used that as fuel to move forward in life. I wanted to prove him wrong.

When we came back to my aunt and uncle's farm this time, we brought Kim. She was still living at home, skinny as all be and unsure of how to live life fully. Like me, she had these loud voices in her head shouting the belief system that was not ours but our father's. Dad was a loud and dominating man full of aggression at the slightest misgiving. Unforgiving and bitter when others around him succeeded, he took to chastising all of his kids. I am not sure what he was like in public to people, but at home he was a jealous man with a chip on his shoulder. Interestingly enough, Dad was skin and bones and only about five feet eight, but what he lacked in size he made up for with a billowing voice.

When it was time to leave, I thanked him and gave him a warm hug. I was truly grateful for the car, and I slid into the driver's seat, keys in the ignition. I drove away with a sense of freedom I had never had before. The Olds was nothing fancy and perhaps not even road safe, but it was my first ticket to freedom.

Kim rode shotgun for the two-and-a-half-hour trip. Now twenty and twenty-two, this was our first road trip together in my very own vehicle. I knew she could no longer live at Dad's either, so we started to devise a plan for her great escape! For us, leaving home wasn't a sentimental moment of sadness and excitement, but rather a mission to save ourselves from a life sentence.

Chapter 26

Working Towards Independence

My first job in Lloydminster was at a clothing store. Unlike the job I held in Saskatoon after I dropped out of college, I actually liked these brand-name clothes that were for people my age, and my co-workers were awesome for the most part. I was so nervous on my first day of work that I had to quickly open the door of the car and throw up my Rice Krispies. My aunt and sister watched me as they were waiting to wave me off—a Baker tradition.

Parallel parking this beast of a vehicle downtown was not my strong suit, so even if I had to park far away, I would find a spot I could drive into. Lucky for me I had mostly day shifts so I didn't have to worry about too many spots being taken by the time I arrived.

It was pouring rain, and as I opened the door to the store and pulled down my hood, I was met with a frenzy of activity. Our storage area roof was leaking, and the owner said we had to get all the boxes of decorations down from there so they didn't get soaked. I hated ladders, but when you're the new kid on the block and in desperate need of money, you do what you're asked. I followed her to the back storage and we came upon the mess of water. The plan was for me to climb the ladder to the storage area and pass the soaking wet boxes down to her. As I grabbed the box above me, I felt surprised and unsteady at the weight of it. The water had weighed it down significantly, and my arms shook as the boxes wobbled in my hands. I lost control and the box tipped, pouring the water that had collected on top of it onto my new boss! She was drenched and I was stunned! Her husband and another worker heard the commotion and rushed to the back to see what was happening. They immediately busted out in laughter! Too shocked to laugh, I climbed down as she wiped the black mascara off her face and shook her hands by her side. *Well, that's the end of this job,* I thought. Instead, she joined in with the others and laughed at how ridiculous the situation was. She warmly patted me on the back and said I'd made quite the splash in my first ten minutes! That comment loosened my funny bone, and I joined in too. We laughed so hard we cried!

I worked my eight-hour day and climbed into the rusty old girl for the drive home. I was feeling more and more independent while working, living in a good place and being surrounded by good people. I knew life was headed in the right direction.

I worked mostly weekdays, leaving me free to tag along with my aunt and uncle to my cousin Emma and her family in Sherwood Park. They had a beautiful new baby, Anna, whom we all adored. Spending time with Anna was one of my favourite things to do. I once again felt like part of a family, but this time I truly was.

I had admired my Emma since I was old enough to form memories. A beautiful blond with a natural way with people, she was someone I aspired to be like. She always included me in family things, and even though we were nine years apart, I felt like we caught up in age once we graduated and were out in the world. When we were kids, she would pay special attention to Kim and me. My aunt would often be tasked with the back-to-school shopping for Kimberley and me, so Emma would come to the mall as well. Her laugh was infectious, and she had a special way of just being who she was, which was the quality I admired the most. She showed me what it meant to be confident, and I loved being around her.

Kim spent a couple of weeks with us, which was just enough time for her, Auntie and me to put the wheels in motion for Kim to move in with our friend Maureen and get a job in Kindersley. My aunt bought a hair kit and did up some beautiful blond highlights in Kim's hair. She was elated when she saw herself in the mirror! Other than her graduation day, I couldn't recall ever seeing Kim that excited, and she looked fantastic!

Next, we updated her resume, which was rather small, printed out several copies. The following weekend I took her home and spent the weekend with her and Maureen. We handed out resumes everywhere from hotels to gas stations in Kindersley. It didn't take long to get her first bite. A job at 7-11 was her ticket off the farm and into independence, just like me! Dad agreed to move her into Maureen's, and just like that she was also on her own with a job! The Kirk girls could do it, we were just a bit slow out of the gate! In our defence, we were never set up for success or treated as equals at home because we were girls. Our dad preferred boys, so we were expected to be good housekeepers, stay skinny and cook well so we could marry rich. It was pretty sad, but we used it as fuel to power our new start in life!

Chapter 27

Services No Longer Required

I liked my job at the clothing store for the most part. I enjoyed the fall fashion show, looking at new lines of clothing, sorting through boxes upon boxes of new arrivals, steaming them and helping customers. It was very similar to my old job in Saskatoon, but this store had a far younger cliental as we carried men's and women's clothing and also hit the age group I was in. Personally, I loved the clothes!

I paid for my gas, my student loan and any other things I needed. It felt good to gain some independence again with the safety net of my aunt and uncle in place. I gained confidence each day as I learned and grew as a person.

Apparently, Kim struggled to wake up and make her shifts, so she lost her job at the 7-11 and was working as a housekeeper at a hotel in Kindersley. She called me for advice, but I didn't know what to do or say, so I spoke with Maureen to see if she was around to wake Kim for her shifts.

A new girl started at the clothing store, and I liked her a lot until I found out she was talking poorly about me behind my back. She became buddy-buddy with our boss, which meant I was no longer buddy-buddy with the boss. I hated to admit it, but I was jealous. She didn't make me work most weekends, and she was just so kind, but all of a sudden my schedule was changed and I saw my name on lots of Saturdays. I didn't know what to do other than complain to other workers behind her back.

A word to the wise: Do NOT complain to the other workers about your boss. After my shift one Thursday, my boss took me aside and told me she would no longer need me. Shocked, I pulled my coat on and left.

The drive back to my aunt's felt long. My thoughts were racing—How could I tell these amazing people who have supported and loved me that I am out of a job? I wondered if they'd be mad at me or make me feel ashamed. Too late, I already felt ashamed and panicked; sick to my stomach really.

As I pulled into their yard, I saw everyone bustling in the kitchen. I turned the car off and took some deep breaths. *Deep breaths,* I think to myself. *Deep breaths.* Walking through their doorway never got old, but I wondered what our conversation would be like once I explained my job loss. I wanted to stay there more than anything, but I was afraid I'd be asked to leave.

Auntie wiped her hands on a towel as she greeted me with a big smile. My tear-stained cheeks full of shame stopped her in her tracks, and she dropped her towel and rushed over to embrace me. I told her I'd been let go—well, laid off or let go, I wasn't sure. All I knew was I no longer had a job. Embracing me tightly she reassured me it would be okay and I'd find another job. My body shuttered in relief, and tears I had managed to keep at bay when I walked in the door flowed freely as my aunt gently held me.

As the rest of the family walked in, Auntie told them my news. They were all instantly on my side, and no one blamed me or made me feel ashamed. I was not mocked or called a loser or stupid. Instead, I was met with love, compassion and reassurance that this was a temporary setback. The first thing I was tasked with is to find out if this was a layoff or if I was actually fired. That was for the next day's to-do list. That night, I sat with my family as they wrapped me in a love and a belief in me I had never experienced.

Chapter 28

One Door Closes, Another One Opens

"Go see Rose for lunch this Wednesday, Diana. She has a lead on a nanny job for a family with two little girls," Auntie said just before she and Uncle left for Bullhead City, Arizona.

So I took the fifteen-minute drive to Rose's farm on Wednesday. She was just the kindest soul and my aunt's best friend. I have known her since I was little, as she and my aunt had met in nursing school. She gave me the name and number of the local family that was looking for a nanny, so I called Lori that afternoon and we arranged a meeting for Friday. By the time we were done our coffee and I'd met the girls, I was hired! My first day of work was on Monday, Valentine's Day!

In the meantime, I'd met a new boyfriend, Brent. He was a kind man, the life of any party he went to. We had been friends for a long time, but we moved to more than friends in January. He lived in Cudworth and was actually friends with my ex. Yeah, maybe not the most conventional idea to date an ex's friend, but Brent was so kind and compassionate. He always put me first and truly cared about me. For the first time in my life (I know, I know, I keep saying that) I had found someone who met my list. He visited me a lot and was a genuinely good person.

For the next four months I was a nanny to two amazing little girls, Alyssa and Mackenzie! They were wonderful, and their sisterhood reminded me of how Kim and I had always been: thick as thieves and at each other's throats all at once. They taught me so much about how beautiful the world can be from a child's eye. We did crafts, laughed and worked through little Mac Attack's (our little nickname for her) night terrors. I laughed at the way she layered bathing suits and then dresses over top, making bathroom time a challenge! Mac and I spent every day together as Alyssa went to kindergarten every other day. We loved meeting the bus when it was Alyssa's turn to be dropped off. We went on nature walks, to the rink for skating practice, and we spent lots of time with their friends they were allowed to have over while I was with them. Even my sister met the girls when she had some time off (which was often as she was still unable to make it to work on time). I loved those two little girls with all my heart, and the family showed me so much acceptance, so much love. I felt joy awaken deep within my soul.

Chapter 29

Learning to Communicate

With each family I spent time with, be it Dave's, my aunt and uncle's, Brent's and the Sand's, I lapped up key things I missed as a child and needed in order to grow up. They all loved one another. They fought, but it wasn't like the fighting I was used to where the parent pits child against child. Unfortunately, this was the case with me and my brother Chris. We could both be stubborn and could get hurt easily as we were sensitive. We then covered up our hurt with anger and yelling. If this family pattern of arguing non-stop and yelling was going to continue, I sensed it would be between us two. Seeing families fight but not escalate to all-out ugly blowouts was refreshing, and it taught me that there was a different way to deal with anger.

One day, I got a phone call from my dad, so when Auntie handed me the phone after talking to him, I sat down to take it in the kitchen.

"Hi, Dad! How are you?" I said cheerily. It wasn't even a fake cheer, I just felt happy!

The voice on the other end of the phone did not greet me with the same enthusiasm. He had been drinking, and my heart deflated. When Dad had been drinking it was hard to hold a clear conversation with him. Heck, when he was sober sometimes I'd wish he was drunk because it could be even harder then! I took a deep breath in before asking how he was doing.

"So are you liking it there still?" he asked. "You know Chris is mad at you. He says you're being stuck up and think you're better than us."

The insults kept coming, so I tried to weed through what was the truth and what wasn't. As much as I knew Chris wasn't always happy with me, I also believed deep down he loved me. When we all lived at the farm, we depended on each other as kids. We had no one else. Chris helped with my asthma once by trying to give me coffee because he had heard it would help open up my airways. It was sweet but didn't work, and I ended up in the hospital. He could also be a joker, pretending a tablespoon of hot sauce was ketchup and enjoying watching my face as I exploded in heat and rage! We also had some regular kid moments like building that fort.

As Dad hurled insults at me fast and furious, I was triggered. He was still angry that I was living with Auntie and Uncle. He was angry that I didn't call enough. He was angry that I was ungrateful for the vehicle. He was angry, so I got angry too! I exploded, tossing insults back at him and calling him out on being drunk. My aunt walked over and motioned me to hang up, so I did. She embraced me in a hug and asked me what happened, so I shared all the scathing things he said about me. While I had told her of these conversations in the past, this was the first time she bore witness to it. She was speechless.

"Diana, I know you are hurt, but getting mad back at your dad is what he wants," she said. "He wants to pull you into his world of fighting, and arguing. He wants you and Chris to fight because he believes this is how a family functions for some reason. It's not. Do I scream at Uncle or my kids? Do I yell insults at them to make them feel worthless? No. That is not what a good parent does. I know he was drinking, which doesn't help, but you have to own your part here too. You may not be able to change his drinking or what he says, but you can certainly change yours. You choose how you react. If he gets a rise out of you, he has achieved his goal; he wins. There is power in staying quiet or choosing your words carefully in a quiet tone rather than yelling back."

Silently Said

I knew she was right. My olive skin usually didn't turn red, but I felt the heat of embarrassment rise to my face. I was ashamed because I realized I had become what I didn't respect in my dad. Auntie's words sank into my mind as she hugged me one more time before I made my way down to the cave.

I pulled out a piece of paper and a pen to write down all the insults my dad said to me. I pondered each of them as I allowed tears from what felt like years of pent-up frustration, hurt and judgement pour out of me. I wrote it all out, and it was as if the tears I cried cleared my vision as I saw the painful words on paper and knew most of them were not true. Dad was just angry. I was not a bad daughter or sister. I was not selfish. I was not stupid for not finishing college. I was not stuck up. I did care about my family, but I was broken and could not be what I once was to my dad, his right-hand girl. I had to be my own person, with dreams and hopes, goals and accomplishments. I had to be who I was meant to be, which was not what he wanted from me. I was twenty years old, but one conversation with my dad could send me back to that little girl who felt like a failure.

I collected my pages of writing and climbed the narrow beige staircase on the west side of the house. I slipped on a jacket and made sure it had a lighter in the pocket. After sliding my farm shoes on, I opened the door, which released a slight creek, and walked outside to the fresh spring air. Clinging to the judgmental words on these sheets, I walked to the burn barrel (every farm has one of these). There was no wind so I knew it is safe to burn. Once there, I shredded up the sheets one by one, tears streaming down my face. I fumbled with the lighter as I dropped most of the torn-up paper into the barrel but kept one aside that I didn't shred. That paper held the harshest words my father said to me. It detailed the failures he threw in my face, the ugliest insults and the cruelest of lies. It detailed his expectations of me and disappointments in me. I broke the silence when I crumpled this paper, flicked the lighter and held the flame to the page. It caught fire, and I watched the words burn as I dropped it into the barrel with the other pages. Right then and there I made a promise to myself:

I can be the change. I can end the cycle of drama by walking away when things get heated. I can at least remain calm. Watching the words become ash in that burn barrel, I sensed a release in my body I hadn't felt before.

As the last of the pages turned to ash, I backed away and turned towards the house. Auntie was watching me from the kitchen window with a smile. She looked curious as I made my way back to the house, this time using the front door. I smelled a little like smoke, but Auntie embraced me as I walked inside. Feelings of unconditional love washed over me. Somehow in her eyes, I could do no wrong, and I relished the feelings of approval and love.

Chapter 30

Littlest Hobo

There was this TV show, *The Littlest Hobo*, that our family watched. This German shepherd dog would trot down a dusty old country road to help rescue people in distress. Somehow, he always managed to save the day! At the end of each episode, the Littlest Hobo would move on down the road, making his way to his next adventure. I felt a "Littlest Hobo" moment coming—*Just keep moving on*, my internal guidance system whispered. It was in the spring of 2000 when I felt this urge coming to me. College was back on the table, and I felt a move was in my future. Healing for the previous year gave me my footing again, and as much as I loved being with my aunt and uncle, I was drawn back to Saskatoon and closer to Brent and my friends.

I applied to an executive assistant course based on my aunt's advice. I wanted to apply to university to go into social work, but she said it would be too depressing. Once I got my letter of acceptance, I let the family I was working for know I would be leaving at the start of July. As much as they were sad to see me go, they supported me, which meant a lot. On my last day of work, we had a little party, enjoyed some time on the trampoline and running around outside, and we had lots of cuddles. It was a great experience being their nanny, and I felt a bond with those girls that I knew I would carry with me for the rest of my life.

I packed up my old car to temporarily move in with a couple of friends while I looked for a place. School started July 11, and I hadn't had time to find anywhere to live. Auntie and Uncle were so good to me for that year and a half we spent together. As hard as it was for them to let me go, they knew it was time as well. I walked up the staircase with my last box of things when Uncle asked me if I had enough gas; he was always taking care of me like that. I replied that I would get some at the Shell once I got to Lloyd and he nodded, then embraced me tightly.

"I love you, Kiddo! You are always welcome back here any time!" he said.

My vision blurred as my eyes welled up and I tried to push the tears back. I was still not overly comfortable crying in front of others. As a child, my way of handling my feelings was to go for a long walk down to the dugout and cry by myself or lock myself in my bedroom for hours. I tried with all my might to keep my tears from meeting someone's eyes.

Auntie was my next goodbye. She followed me outside with a sandwich and a pop for the trip, and I placed my box into the trunk of my car. Auntie was considerate like that, and she knew I did not have much money until my student loan kicked in. We walked back to the covered patio and sat for a bit, chatting about all the exciting things yet to come. Both of us were trying to focus on the positive, knowing this was the next good step in my future, but we both felt the emotions that separation from those you love conjures up. It wasn't lost on me that this was how one should feel when they leave home: excited, scared and a bit morose. It was hard to leave the people and the place that helped me heal. There was safety in these four walls that held my heart and soothed my soul, but I had grown as much as I could there and it was time to venture out on my own. I was twenty one years old, and it felt like I was leaving home for the first time.

My aunt and I shared a long embrace before I walked to my junky old car, which is home to more rust than when I got it. I hadn't washed it since I bought it—terrible I know—because it's so full of holes I knew I would leave more of the car in the carwash than mud!

My aunt, who wasn't overly mushy, pulled away, held my shoulders and said she believed in me. She said she knew I could do this, that I was a smart, capable young lady and not to listen to anyone who told me different. She pulled me in for one last hug, and I walked to my car.

The feeling of leaving that place brought me back to that little girl Diana who loved to lap up all the attention the people gave me there. I was brought back to the sadness of having to go back to our family farm as a child and how hard I tried to push those tears back into my broken little heart. I felt very much the same longing to stay in the perfect world we created there, but I had to follow my intuition and strike out into the unknown. As I slid my car into reverse and backed up, I saw Auntie and Uncle standing on the deck with their arms wrapped around each other's waists. *I want that kind of love*, I thought to myself. They waved as I drove down their laneway and onto my next adventure. This was what it feels like to leave home; this was what love and family should be.

Chapter 31

Take Two

My first day of college went well, and we learned we would focus on self-development for the first three days. I was curious what this would be like, but as timing is always divine, I quickly lapped up the idea of positive affirmations, leaving old belief systems behind and focusing on the task at hand: to graduate college and start a career that will lead to success.

Knowing I had to find a place to live, I turned to the classified section of *The Star Phoenix*, our local paper in Saskatoon, and circled a few ads. I wanted to move in with someone who was not a friend. Staying with my friends temporarily was already feeling a bit tense because I was sleeping on their pull-out couch in the living room. I felt misplaced and knew I needed a place to call my own by August 1, so I set that goal.

A week into my time in Saskatoon, I found an ad that appealed to me, so I called the girl up and we planned to meet that Thursday evening. Kerri was a single mom with the most adorable two-year-old I had ever met! When I walked into their duplex, I was greeted with the biggest smile I'd seen on such a small child! I immediately knew this was home.

We toured around and she showed me where I could sleep. We discussed rent, food and what would work for us both. We would share everything. Anything in the fridge that either of us bought would be for us both. We could even grocery shop together if we wanted to, but she said her parents liked to buy lots of food for them, so we could just eat what they buy, and I wouldn't be expected to pay for that. I couldn't believe what I was hearing. The place was spacious, in a good neighbourhood and not too long of a bus ride or car ride to the downtown campus. Kerri was in university, too, and, ironically, taking social work. My best friend Lindsay was also taking social work and lived not too far from Kerri's place, so things fell into place nicely!

On August 1, Brent and I moved my meager belongings into the duplex. Kerri was gone for the weekend, so we made ourselves at home. When I went to preheat the oven to make us pub food for supper, I decided to open it up first, which I never did before preheating. It was a good thing I did, as I was greeted by a pile of dirty dishes! Kerri hadn't had time to clean up too much before she left for the weekend, and I guess she stuck the dishes in the oven! In her defence, we did not have a dishwasher. Brent and I had a good chuckle over this.

I worked hard in school for the next several months and made some new friends, one who was very smart and seemed to be a high achiever. My aunt told me to hang out with people who are successful because it pushes you to be the same. Renee was really smart, and since taking that first week of learning how to think right in school, I felt that maybe if I applied myself, I, too, could be really smart!

On our first day of college, a professional speaker came in to help us all realign our thoughts about school. There were many younger people, like me, but also single moms and older students. We all had one thing in common: to make a better life for ourselves.

"Forget your grades in high school. They don't matter here," he said. "The only thing that matters here is what you think and how you handle those thoughts. You can do anything you set your mind to, but you must be focused. You must work at it. You must find the place within yourself that burns with the desire to win. I say this isn't high school because now you are out of the social settings and expectations friends and peer groups bring. Those relationships can be great or weigh you down. You are all strangers here—make friends. Learn and lift each other up. Raise your own bar and amaze yourself. If I believe in you and I'm a complete stranger, you should be able to believe in yourselves."

These words hit differently that day. As an average to below average student, I saw an opportunity to grow, and I wanted it. I didn't want to be broke or have a bad career. I wanted to surpass my father's labels and move myself forward. That day, I vowed to get on the honour role, something I had never achieved.

At the end of the year, both Auntie and the motivational people were correct. I'd earned straight A's by the end of the year. The only thing I changed that year was my thoughts about who I was.

In January, my aunt and uncle had gone down south again for a few months so they could skip the bitter cold of our brutal prairie winters. Brent and I celebrated our one-year anniversary by going out to a restaurant and enjoying some drinks with friends. On Sunday, I received a call from my aunt. There was panic in her voice and my mind raced in fear.

"Diana, I have some bad news," she said, and my heart sank. "First off, I want you to know we are fine, your family is fine, this is nothing to do with your family."

I wanted to feel relief, but the sound of her voice did nothing to reassure me.

"Mackenzie passed away this morning at her home."

The words came at me like thunder. I did not understand.

"No one knows what caused it, but she is gone. Alyssa was at a sleepover. Lori was making some snacks for a church event when she heard Mackenzie in distress. David, her dad, tried to save her, but it was too late."

I buckled under the weight of her words as my world collapsed into darkness. I did not understand. Surprisingly, before I moved away, Lori announced she was expecting their third child in October. Mackenzie turned four in November. It was the end of January, so baby Payton was in the picture, Alyssa was in Grade 1 and Mackenzie was gone! Life reminded me, yet again, of how fleeting it can be.

I went to school the next day and had to leave class several times in tears. My professor asked me if anything was wrong so I shared the sad news. Everyone was very understanding and promised to catch me up as I had to miss a couple of days to go back to Lloydminster to attend the funeral. Brent came with me for support.

Walking into the small-town church, I was greeted with pictures and artwork of Mackenzie's, much of it we had done together. Overcome with emotion, we found a seat. I had spoken with Lori a couple of times during the week; no one could make sense of what had happened. She had asked that I come to the graveyard after, which we did. Brent stayed in the car as I stood there watching her be laid to rest. The family had received permission to bury Mackenzie over top of her grandma since she was just a small child. It was a beautiful gesture. Right then and there I made a deal with God that if he gave me a daughter, her middle name would be Mackenzie.

Chapter 32

Stepping into Normal

The school year wore on, and Brent and I started to make plans for the future. This guy was the real deal: kind, caring and compassionate. He loved me and put me ahead of everything. We spent weekends together and talked about moving in together. I wanted to move back to Lloyd to be closer to my family, but he had a good job in St. Brieux. There seemed to be good opportunities there for me as well, but it was a good six hours away from Lloyd, and being that far away from my solid base was not something I wanted.

"Diana, I just got on through on C95's game!" Kerri yelped as she barged into the bathroom with a cordless phone, one hand covering the receiver.

I laughed while rinsing conditioner out of my hair.

"Diana, get out of the shower, I can't do it! You have to!"

"What?!" I yelled back as my eyes widen.

"Get out of the shower now!"

I did as I was instructed, quickly wrapped one towel around my small frame and another around my soaking wet hair. I threw on my glasses, confused at the situation.

"Diana, I can't do this! You have to! We can split the prize, just take the phone!"

She thrust the phone in front of me, receiver covered with one hand, and I heard a voice on the other end. It was the radio DJ, which meant it was go time! I was freaking out a little too. The announcer asked if it was Kerri on the phone, and I explained it was her roommate, Diana, and she got me out of the shower to play this game! We shared a laugh then he explained that I had to answer a series of questions correctly in order to advance to the final survival round the following Friday. If I answered two out of three questions correctly, I won some CDs, movie tickets and other coupons as well as advancing to the next round where the prize was a five-hundred-dollar shopping spree to a sports/outdoors store! I hadn't bought a new winter jacket since 1994 (which means I hadn't grown since then either). Soaking wet with only a towel wrapped around my body, I managed to win the game! Good thing the questions were all trivia related to *Survivor*, which happened to be my favourite show on TV! Kerri and her little boy listened to me in her bedroom so as not to confuse me when I was on the radio. The DJ said they would call next Friday for the final round and that all semi-finalists were automatically invited to their *Survivor* party at the Sutherland Bar!

Kerri and Carter came barrelling out of her bedroom when I was off air, cheering and excited for me. This was not the way I had planned on starting my day considering I wasn't even trying to get into the contest. At school, a number of the teachers and students asked if I was on the radio that morning, and I got a kick out of telling the story.

When Friday rolled around again I was far more nervous. More of my friends knew, and everyone was going to tune in to the finals between the five of us who had advanced. I made it to the final round against a man, and we had to plead our case as to why we needed the shopping spree more. I told them I was a poor student just trying to start out in life while looking for a job. The person I was against said he had a young child at home and planned to buy her some winter clothes. I knew he needed it more than me, and the radio listeners voted for him, but it didn't matter. I was glad he could clothe his child, and I was pretty happy to have played. We were just about done when the DJ said someone called in to offer me a job! I was shocked! I thanked them so much but explained that I would be moving to

St. Brieux and planned to work closer to my boyfriend. The world was certainly full of surprises!

That was also the final day to get my typing score up to sixty words per minute so I could graduate. It was the same thing that hooked me last time I took a similar course, but I was riding the high of the radio show and nothing could knock me down, so I walked into the computer lab like I owned the place, My fingers danced across the keyboard at a time of seventy-four words per minute, so with a few typos, I achieved sixty-seven words per minute. I had completed what I set out to do, and man did that feelt good! With a score like that I knew I had the course in the bag, and I could taste the hard work paying off.

I graduated college, with honours, in May, which was something I never in my wildest dreams thought possible. As the trainers had said on our first day of school, this was a chance to make something more for myself—that the world was ours to capture and mould. They were right. I heeded this advice and found success. I walked across the stage with my dad, Brent, his parents, Auntie Betty and Uncle Walt, Uncle Perry and Auntie Daisy in the audience cheering me on.

Afterwards we all went for supper. My dad and Auntie Betty were talking about how proud they were of me and how it was a joint effort to get me to where I was. I had never felt my dad was proud of me, and I liked the warmth it imprinted on my heart; it made me want to keep making him proud.

Auntie Betty once gave me some great advice: "You may not believe in yourself, but I believe in you; borrow that until you do. I have enough belief in you for the both of us." I carried those words with me knowing that I owed this second chance, this change in my life, to my aunt, uncle and their family. They took me in when I was lost, broke, scared and newly single. I was a real fixer-upper, and she could see potential in me that I did not. Sometimes after we've been beaten down and battered, we don't see that we are only tarnished. The shine we show others comes from our souls, and no matter how broken I felt, I knew I could depend on my aunt and uncle. They took the time to really see me, and I borrowed their belief in me long before I had any of my own.

Chapter 33

On the Move

Moving to St. Brieux and into Brent's small basement suite did not scare me in the least. It was more than adequate for what we needed, and we moved into a larger two-bedroom apartment soon after. After completing a two-week internship at Bourgualt Industries, which was where Brent worked, I was disheartened to hear I would not be hired. However, it did not take long for the small town to jump into action, and I got a call from Dryair Manufacturing at Brent's parents' house asking if I wanted a job as an administrative assistant. I said yes, and she told me to come in on Monday. I didn't know if that meant I had the job or just an interview, but it turned out that I had the job and Monday was my first day!

Working full time at Dryair was good for me. I did the regular administrative assistant duties and kept very busy. It was a manufacturing company, and the team in the back was young, like me. Soon Brent and I got in with a social crowd and embarked on an active social life! I felt I had achieved a "normal" life, which was all I set out to do, and it was blissful.

It wasn't meant to last for long, though, as I got a call from Kim. She had recently moved home because she could not keep a job.

"Diana, I can't handle it here anymore," Kim said, weeping on the other end of the phone.

Dad had gone to the bar, so she grabbed the cordless phone off the wall between the kitchen and dining room and brought it to her bedroom. Aaron was also living at home, but he was farming with Dad. Kim was helping with the pigs and other farm chores.

"Kim, what's wrong?" I asked.

For a girl who said few words, she chronicled the stress she was under for about half an hour before I could get a word in. Dad's drinking was out of control. She had her license but no car, and he wouldn't let her have it so she couldn't go anywhere. All she did was sit in her room all day and draw or spend time with the animals. When dad was around, he demanded that she does this or that.

"I am not his slave, Diana! I can't take this!"

I want to cry for her. I challenged her to stand up to him and put her foot down, but she resisted.

"I have no power here, Diana. Can't you see that? I take it because I have nowhere to go."

My thoughts flew out of my mouth as fast as I could think them, and I said, "Come move in with us! We just moved to a bigger apartment with two bedrooms, and you can have one. There are lots of jobs around here. We have tons of friends and have lots of fun! Come live here, Kim. We can help you."

It occurred to me that I hadn't spoken to Brent this about, but I was sure he would warm up to the idea even if he wasn't totally keen to begin with. I could almost hear the smile spread across her face when she quietly said, "Really? Can I? You'd let me stay with you?"

"Yes!" I replied confidently. "We will handle this. We will help you. You deserve to be as happy as I am. You can't be stuck on the farm with no friends or social life other than when my childhood friend Maureen comes home on a weekend here and there. You are not someone's slave! There are plenty of single guys here with good jobs, and maybe you can find someone!"

I was even more excited than her as I started to daydream out loud about all the things we could do together, the places she could apply and how wonderful life could be!

"Brent could drop me off at work, or I could take him, then you can use my car to get to your job!"

Brent's dad took pity on me and my car in May and bought me a far better used car. It had no rust and was in great shape. It was a comfortable 1994 Chevy Celebrity that was eight years newer and half the size of my old, rusty Oldsmobile. She was a dream vehicle compared to what I had! Brent's dad sold my old car so I didn't feel as bad taking a new car. I thought he would keep the money, but he knew we were young and just starting out, so he told me to keep it. So kind!

Kim sounded far more hopeful at the end of our conversation.

"The only thing I will miss about this place is spending time with Gizmo, my niece, Breanna's dog. They moved to a place that doesn't allow dogs, so dad took him in," Kim said.

All animals loved Kim.

My conversation with Brent about Kim moving in didn't go over quite as I hoped, and he was not overly receptive at first. All of his siblings lived on their own, had their jobs and found their way.

"Brent, Kim is my sister! I know your brothers are way older than you and that you didn't grow up the same way as I did, but I will not abandon her!" I pleaded with him.

There were sixteen years between the youngest and the oldest in his family, all boys and all great people with good families. He doesn't understand because he didn't grow up in a household that was deeply filled with trauma.

"If you don't want her here, then I will move into my own place and help her!" I said. "You don't understand how we grew up—there is no option not to help, it's what we do. We don't leave anyone behind. We had to rely on each other so much that we know we can always count on each other to get through. She honestly will not survive! I know her. If she is this upset now, she is at the end of her rope! I refuse to stand by and do nothing! Everyone ran away on us and left us to take care of our mom and ourselves when we were kids, and I will never turn my back on my siblings! The four of us got through this together, no walking away, no choices. This is a no-brainer, and if it comes down to you or her, it's her!"

My case was a bit harsh, but the situation was dire.

Brent looked like I'd just run over him with a freight train. All the colour was gone from his face as he looked at me with deep remorse. I'd shared some of the trauma we went through as children, but he hadn't seen the bond that blossomed out of the ashes of our childhood. I could help her just like Auntie helped me, and I went to our bedroom to wait until he came to his senses.

"You're right, Diana, she can live with us," Brent said as he timidly pushed open the door and scanned the room for me. "We will help. We will not leave her behind. I may not have grown up like you, but I sure as hell can see it left its share of scars. I've never seen you so upset."

"That's because I get mamma bear protective over my sister—I always have. She can't stand up for herself, so I do it for her. I am her voice. She says things with her silence and not everyone can hear her, but I can."

Chapter 34

Three's Company

Kimberley was giddy with excitement and ridden by guilt all at the same time. Us Kirks are all plagued with this feeling: happy for ourselves when we finally get rescued and sad for those we leave in the mess. The one left behind this time was the little dog Gizmo. We all had strong attachments to animals, and we had kittens and a dog for as long as I had been around. Sometimes it wasn't our dog at the farm but someone else's who couldn't have it at their place. Dad had a soft spot for animals too.

We made the four-hour drive back to St. Brieux with Kimberley and all her belongings, which, just as when I left home, was pretty much the contents of her bedroom. We gave her the basement so she could set up a whole space down there to herself. We offered the second bedroom, but it had our computer and she felt the basement would be better. It wasn't finished, but there was lots of space. I must admit, her meagre belongings tucked in the corner of that big basement made the little she had stand out, so we tucked a rocking chair, a little area rug and another lamp down there.

We shared celebratory drinks and lots of good laughs that night. As my eyes met hers, she spoke with her silence yet again, and I heard her heart, her soul. *Thank you for saving me. I love you.* Words have always been my thing, not Kim's, and I couldn't get so much as a hug from this girl unless I held her down and forced her (you know, sisterly love!). Breaking our gaze with a big smile, I felt hopeful for her future. I would do what I could to help her because she had no one else.

When Kim moved into our condo in May, we went through our initial honeymoon phase. We hadn't lived together since 1998, and we were both happy to spend evenings watching TV, making suppers and cleaning up. She had some money saved up but didn't have much interest in working. She threw her resume out to a few places, but it wasn't a very good one because she couldn't keep a job. So she spent her days in our condo watching TV and enjoying drawing in her sketchbook.

One evening after cleaning up dishes she said, "You know when I moved to Lethbridge to go to art school?"

"Uh yeah, kinda hard to forget. I was in Grade 12. We moved you in August of 1995. What about it?"

My feet switched places as I stood like a flamingo, leaning against the white Arborite countertop. Raising my brow in curiosity, her gaze fell to the floor. She wouldn't look at me, and it was like she was arguing with herself to tell me something.

"What about it?" I prodded.

"Well ..."

She tilted her head as she stared at the towel she was wringing tightly between her milky white hands—hands just like our mother's, with lean, boney fingers and blood vessels protruding aggressively. Her skin was so pale it was almost translucent. She was also very skinny. My sister-in-law brought her weight to my attention several times, but I sluffed it off because she was built exactly like our mother, skin and bones. With a deep breath, Kim plunged into recounting the year she spent in Lethbridge.

"Diana, I didn't go to school. I spent most of my days pretending like I went, but I would sit in a park nearby and pass the time watching nature. I went the first couple of days, got some textbooks, but I was so lonely and scared. I didn't know what to do. I struggled to get out of bed. I was so worried my landlord would tell Dad."

Her landlord was the eldest daughter of that nice grain elevator agent I told you about in an earlier chapter.

"I was so scared, and I didn't know what to do, so I did nothing."

I slid my leg back down to the ground to gain my footing.

"Why didn't you call me? I could have helped you tell Dad or get a plan together. You didn't have to do this alone, Kim."

I knew she had failed out of university, but I didn't realize she didn't actually attend class. Most of us new to living on our own struggle to motivate ourselves to get to class, especially after spending thirteen years in school!

"I had to tell you; I felt so guilty keeping it from you. Dad paid for it, and I wasted it."

This had been a sore spot for me. Dad had paid for everyone to do something. Aaron got four years of University, Kim one year, and Chris got a nice truck, but by the time I was ready to fly the nest, there was next to nothing left except for the actual land, and he needed that to keep an income. I felt forgotten about and not worth spending a dime on. Hearing her recount her story, I had to remember this was not about me, so I placed my bitterness back in the box.

"Diana, you know how I'm dyslexic, right? Well, things are just harder than they should be with that, especially school. And I have a hard time working."

I suggested we move the conversation to her area of the condo so she could be comfortable with her things around her. Kim wasn't one to open up, and I didn't want to scare her with an audience of people or the distraction of *Friends* on the TV. As we sat on her tightly-made bed, I felt the weight of my body sink into her purple ombre comforter.

"Diana, I don't know if I can work. I'm not really good at anything. Things are hard for me. I don't know why."

As I took in her words, a thought came to mind.

"Maybe you should go on social assistance for a bit, just until we can sort things out. I'm also going to get in touch with a few places to get your dyslexia tested again. Maybe it's gotten worse."

I promised her we would sort this out and told her not to worry about finding a job until we figured out what was going on.

I made a few phone calls the next day. I had a few friends who were social workers, which helped. My bestie Lindsay worked for social services and put me in touch with the Melfort Office so we can get Kim some help.

Chapter 35

Trust the Process

With step one completed by the social worker, Kim had a small source of income to help cover bills. Going on social assistance wasn't something I wanted for her but feeding another person on my very small wage with no offer of help from my dad meant it was the only way. Until we sorted out what was going on, it would have to do.

A social worker named Shannon, from Melfort, came to our place to assess Kim's needs and referred us to an organization in Saskatoon for some basic aptitude tests, so I took some days off work to take her there. When we next sat down with the social worker, we were surprised at the results.

"Kim, what year did you say you graduated high school?" Shannon questioned.

"1995," she said, beaming with pride.

This was no small feat for the girl as she struggled her way through most of her school years. She had a wonderful teacher assistant that worked with her most days in the resource room, and we were all proud of her hard work and determination to graduate.

Kim went to the basement for a bit while the social worker and I spoke one-on-one.

"You would never know with these tests that your sister graduated high school, let alone got into university. It is no wonder she struggles to hold down a job. Dyslexia is just one part of her learning issues. The school should have seen this and helped her."

"She's never been good at taking tests," I said a bit defensively on Kim's behalf. "In the resource room the teacher could read the test to her, so maybe that improved her scores."

"To be quite frank, Diana, it would not matter if this test was taken orally or written because it's a series of behaviours and aptitudes they test. She needs some assistance. Is there a family history of learning or developmental issues?"

"No," I quickly responded, again with that defensive tone lacing my tongue.

I like this lady, but I am unsure what she is getting at.

"Well, we need a plan. Unfortunately, the rural areas aren't great help when it comes to places for people with developmental issues to work. You may want to consider moving her to Saskatoon where there are facilities that can employ her. Her scores aren't low enough on the charts that she needs full time supervision, but a group home setting would be nice so she isn't alone and can be with people who are on her level."

"Her level?" I thought I asked it in my mind but realized it slipped from my tongue.

"Yes, Diana. Her level. It will limit what she can and cannot do for employment. I am going to put you in touch with a couple of organizations in Saskatoon that should be able to help you out. Community Living Association may be able to help you find housing, and the Saskatchewan Abilities Council employs many people in a few of their locations, including Cosmos Industries. She can keep busy doing tasks such as cleaning, cooking, mending and washing coveralls for places like SaskPower that contract them out to work. Kim can make money doing this, and her assistance cheque would not be affected. She will need to stay on assistance now, as she is unable to work a conventional job."

My head hung low at the heaviness of her words.

"It's OK, Diana. There are great places like the ones I mentioned that can help you out. She can keep some independence while contributing to society. It can be very fulfilling!"

She again asked about family history of illness. Sharing my mom's illness with people was uncomfortable for me for a few reasons, but mostly because we did not have a name for it. Explaining what was happening to her brain when I really didn't understand it myself made it difficult to relay to others.

"If you took a bunch of neurological disorders and lumped them into one disease, that would be what Mom has," I said.

I was unphased by the look on the social worker's face because I had shared my mother's prognosis with people a lot, and I was always met with that exact same look: bewildered with a mix of pity.

"How old was she when she got sick?" she asked.

"She was twenty-six. I was nine months old when she was diagnosed. Her brain was shrinking, and my dad called it a disease of the central nervous system. I don't know a lot about the inner workings of the illness, but I do know what it did to my mom. It took away all her skills. She couldn't write or read, couldn't walk, talk, feed herself. She was pretty much trapped in her body. I have no idea if she knows us or not, she can't share. Sometimes she gets excited. She went into a home when I was very young and hated it when we would leave. In fact, she would scream for hours."

I stopped, knowing I'd overwhelmed her with information. She fiddled with her fingers, much like Grandma Kirk would do; Dad called it twiddling thumbs. Finally, she broke the silence.

"I think maybe Kim should have a physical. She is very thin. Maybe even a neurological examination."

Unphased and not really catching on to what she truly meant, I said, "I'll make Kim an appointment with my doctor in Melfort; he's really nice. Kim hasn't spent a night in the hospital ever! She always bugged me because I have bad asthma, and as a kid I spent lots of time in the hospital. Kim is skinny, and maybe they could figure out what is going on."

The social worker nodded as Kim came up from the basement. She was smiling, apparently unphased by our conversation. After the social worker left, Kim looked at me inquisitively and said, "What is happening to me?" With no real answers, I simply said, "I don't know, but we will find out."

As I sat alone in my room, I sense my discomfort with the conversation the social worker and I had. The overwhelming weight of caregiving was setting in. I had to keep going, but I feared the deeper we dove into this, the more anxious I would become. I could not settle in my skin, I felt sick to my stomach, and my heart all but dropped when I looked in those beautiful, deep blue eyes that aren't just Kimberley's but also my mother's.

Chapter 36

Neurological Testing

With a family history such as ours, doctors are usually curious and confused. I think the no-name part got to them. Kim and I sat on black chairs, side by side, waiting to see my doctor.

"Don't get too distracted with how good looking he is when you see him. He's pretty dreamy!" I said. "He went to school with my chiropractor from Lloyd, who is also super hot!"

Kim shot a two-dimple-wide mischievous grin and we were both giggling when the assistant walked in.

"Kimberley Kirk? The doctor will see you now."

Bouncing up from our chairs in the waiting room, we looked at each other. I didn't know what our looks said—it's hard to put words to it—but I knew how it felt: anxious, nervous mixed with some fear. *Here we go*, I thought as my stomach churned. I am afraid, but of what?

Kim was directed to slide herself onto the cold metal bed covered with a thin sheet of paper. She sat up waiting for the doctor while I searched for a chair to sit on. The air hung heavy with anticipation. This was the first time we've experienced a complete role reversal because I was usually on the bed and someone else was accompanying me. It was a different vantage point being the caregiver rather than the patient.

As the doctor walked in, I shifted my weight from one hip to the other. My hands felt hot and my heart was racing.

"Well, ladies, what can I do for you?"

Kim looked to me for direction, so I piped up as I always had.

"My sister Kim here is really skinny. The social worker told us she should see a doctor," I said, my voice shaking.

"How do you sleep, Kimberley?"

"Pretty good," she replied.

This was a lie. I was baffled, so I tilted my head to the left and continued to observe.

"How have you been feeling?"

"Great since I moved in with my sister!" she answered while he checked her reflexes.

I noted that they seemed slow, and it made me want to check my own as I wonder if they were supposed to be that slow.

"Touch your nose with your index finger, then touch mine," the doctor instructed.

She started with her right hand and shakily made her way to her own nose.

"Now to mine," the doctor encouraged.

Shaking and concentrating heavily, she slowly moved her hand from her nose to his in a very unsteady line, if you could even call it a line. I was surprised. The doctor smiled warmly at her and asked her to wait in the other room while he had a chat with me privately. I was still unsure of what I saw happen but sluffed it off as nerves.

The doctor, always warm and friendly, sat down on a chair in front of me, a gesture I appreciated. As if searching for the right words, his eyes darted around the room; it was the look I make when I'm feeling awkward.

"Diana, I am recommending an MRI for Kim. She failed the neurology exam. Can you tell me about your mom's illness?"

I was quick to share that Kim had a learning disability and that was probably why she failed this exam.

"Diana, what's wrong with your mother?" he asked again softly. "How old was she when she got sick?"

Reluctantly, I shared what I knew. Listening intently, he confirmed that the right course of action was an MRI.

"The wait is very long in this province, probably going to be at least a year," he said. "It's good to have her on the list and maybe if there is a cancellation, she could get in sooner."

"What do you think is wrong?" I found myself asking without actually wanting an answer.

His voice was smooth with compassion when he said, "Something, but I don't really know. We need the MRI to know what is happening in her brain. Keep an eye on things, and if they progress, come see me."

With that I walked out the door to face my sister in the waiting room, unsure what just happened. When Kim asked what he said, I told her we needed an MRI to see what was happening to her brain from the learning disabilities. It was a half-lie, half-truth, but I didn't even know what to think or say, so how would she process it all?

"OK, that makes sense."

She seemed content and not at all thrown off by the appointment. As we pulled out of the clinic parking lot, she reminded me I promised we would have subs for supper, so instead of heading home straight away, we drove towards Subway. Looking over at her, I noticed she was smiling and seemingly content. I was not.

Chapter 37

A Place to Call Home

"We found her a place she can work, Diana!" the social worker said over the phone. I can hear her smile. "SaskAbilities! You just need to meet with their social workers and get things set up."

"OK, but we can't get her into a group home to live. Will she be OK on her own?" I inquired.

"Well, perhaps a basement suite would be good for her, with someone upstairs so she is not alone. You would need to tell them what's going on, and if they're willing to help, then maybe it will work. It would be best if it was within walking distance of SaskAbilities. See what you can find and get back to me. I'll also be transferring Kim's case to Saskatoon if she moves there. There are many capable and compassionate workers with SaskAbilities; I know she will be in good hands."

As I hung up the phone, Kim silently crept up beside me.

"Good news?" she asked with a giddy grin.

"How do you feel about your own place in Saskatoon and working with SaskAbilities?"

Her grin expanded as a full body yes.

"What's SaskAbilities?"

"You know, I'm not entirely sure, but I think we should find out! Your social worker has arranged for us to go there and meet with a social worker, tour the place and see if it's a fit for you. You could work there and stay on social assistance but keep a bit of a wage. We could find you a basement suite with some people living upstairs maybe. Brent and I could visit every weekend, and you would have a place of your very own!"

The thrill in her eyes when those words danced into her ears was something I had rarely seen, like Christmas morning when she got the Barbie she wanted me to ask Santa for. For the first time in a long while, I felt something warm and cozy too: hope.

The next week we drove the smooth pavement of Highway 41 to our appointment at SaskAbilities with a social worker. They would do an intake assessment, determine if she could live alone and if there was any way she could work for them.

"Hi, I'm Dan, your social worker! Nice to meet you guys! Lets get better acquainted, then if I feel this is a match for us and you feel it is for you, we can tour around. How does that sound?"

We both nod in agreement. Kim hasn't stopped smiling since we told her she may get her own place. The idea that she could be independent had her walking on a cloud, so I hoped things wouldn't change after Dan completed his assessment.

Dan was warm and kind, and after the interviewing process was complete I determined the whole place felt the same. She could cook and clean in the kitchen or do washing and mending in the laundry. There was a wood working area and all kinds of other facilities that she could try her hand at. What I saw and felt in this place was more opportunities than I had ever seen before. She could be independent, have a life, make a bit of extra money and have registered social workers close by for six to eight hours a day. Now if we could find her a place within walking distance, we'd have it made in the shade!

Chapter 38

Break Free

Kim first broke free of the farm in the spring when she moved in with Brent and me. On October 1, we moved her into a cute little basement suite only a few blocks away from SaskAbilities. The owners, a younger couple who seemed very kind, lived upstairs with a new baby. We found this ad in the paper, and it was clearly meant to be!

Kim had some money saved which covered the damage deposit along with some new essential items. The two of us could hardly contain our excitement as we pushed our cart through Walmart, heading for the home décor section.

"I need some art!" Kim exclaimed.

Art had become her tool to cope with the stress of our overbearing father and chaotic childhood, and we found a Monet print that spoke to her.

"See how when you're far away like we are, it looks perfect? Then when you get closer, you see the strokes of the brush and it doesn't look as good? I love that about his art—he paints it close up, but it is best viewed from afar."

Not knowing much about art, I could see what she meant. "Yes, that is so cool!"

She picked it up and gently placed it in the cart. Next, we hit up the bathroom section for some towels and a bath-mat and then over to the kitchen area to get a few essentials. The great thing about this place was it was furnished! She only really needed to bring her bed and dresser.

Back at our condo, we packed up Kim's corner of the basement and loaded everything between Brent's dad's truck and my car. I was grateful it wasn't snowing so we wouldn't have bad roads and ice to deal with. Conversation between Kim and I was light as we drove towards Saskatoon.

"Dad was sure surprised to hear that I've got a job with SaskAbilities and my own place, wasn't he?" Kim asked, a hit of giggle in her voice.

"Yes, he sure was! I knew you could do this, Kim! You just needed someone to believe in you like Auntie Betty did for me a few years ago."

I smiled at her and could see the pride spread across her face and dance in her eyes. The excitement of accomplishment couldn't be contained.

"My bedroom is perfect, Diana!" Kimberley squealed in delight as we put the finishing touches on it. "Everything has its place!"

Order and organization had always been Kim's strong suit, unlike me. I was tidy and put things away, but she thought things through before putting the item away and made sure its placement was just right.

Standing at the bottom of the basement stairs, Kim and I hugged goodbye. This was a big moment for her.

"Remember, your landlords said if you need anything, help with anything or whatever, that they are just upstairs, so just knock," I said. They offered to check on Kim and watch out for her. "We will be back Saturday to spend the day with you. Or we can come Friday after work and we can spend the weekend either at Brent's parents' or in St. Brieux."

"Sounds great!"

The time having Kim in our place had been good, but she needed to find her place in the world. It wasn't a conventional way, but after months of testing and planning, we were finally on the right path. We had the right people in place to help, and we understood some of what she was dealing with. She was on the wait list for an MRI (which was a year and a half long), and unless something more showed up, we were assured by the social workers that being on her own was OK. She wasn't bad enough to live in a group home setting, yet not well enough to work a regular job. If we didn't advocate for her, she could have easily fallen through the cracks and just become another statistic of someone who was receiving assistance but that people think can work. She couldn't have a regular job, but her work at SaskAbilities would fill up her days and create new friendships. Dad said she would never amount to anything, never be independent, and we just proved him wrong. It feels great!

Chapter 39

Breakdown

Work for the month of October was busy. I moved from the front desk to the research and development team and began learning how to be a drafting technician. There was a steep learning curve, but if I knew anything about myself it was that I enjoyed learning and a challenge. When I moved into R&D, I was surrounded by a team of guys that were so great! We had lots of fun and yet got our work done. My office was upstairs, and I didn't have to answer the phone, which I liked. My bosses were great; patient with me as I learned the drafting program and how to "explode" out drawings to help the guys in the manufacturing shop use them to put the pieces together. It was kind of like putting a puzzle together then showing step by step how to do it.

The start of November proved to be just as busy, but I had established a routine in my new position. I took a course in Saskatoon which helped me learn the ins and outs of the software program and how to use it for my job, so I spent my day in a classroom with a bunch of other newbies in training. The day was good but felt long. Thankfully, it was a Thursday and *Friends* was on in the evening.

I debated stopping at Kim's place, but it had started to snow and the roads were slick with ice, so I decided to go home. We had picked her up and brought her to Cudworth to hang out with Brent's parents and our friends the last couple of weekends. She seemed happy, work was going well and she was getting to know the people. She usually worked in the kitchen and kept busy. She was enjoying her space but may have been a bit lonely. As I drove the icy highway towards St. Brieux, visibility was reduced, so I was focused on the road and getting back to our warm condo. I pulled into the garage at the back of our building hoping my slushy car would thaw overnight.

I was drained after the white-knuckle drive, and I dragged myself down the long hall to our door, which somehow felt longer that day. I was daydreaming of a nice bath, then curling up with a blanket and my favourite TV show when I walked in to see Brent in the kitchen.

"Weather is shit!" I exclaimed, as if he didn't already know.

"Yeah, and you didn't take the cell phone, I was worried."

We embraced, and I told him my grand evening plans.

"Supper will be ready in twenty minutes," he said. "It's Hamburger Helper."

Oh great, I thought, *I love hamburger helper*—NOT! I kept these thoughts to myself as I was grateful that supper was made; one less thing to do.

As I sank into the tub, Brent yelled, "Hey, Kim's social worker from SaskAbilities called. He said to call him back."

"What did he want?" I yelled back.

"Not sure, just said to call him. He left his cell phone number."

I debated getting out of the warm and soothing bath but decided against it and laid back, letting the water wash over my head, cover my ears and drown out the world. *Now what?* I thought as I tossed around ideas of what Dan wanted.

I pulled myself up from my comforting hot bath then wrapped myself in a towel when the phone rang. Brent answered it and called for me. Covering the receiver, he quietly let me know it was Dan. Frustrated that a new episode of *Friends* was starting shortly and I might miss it, I begrudgingly took the receiver. It was almost like I didn't want to deal with whatever this was, yet I knew I had to be responsible and just find out what was going on.

Politely and with fake cheer, I popped into conversation with Dan and apologized for not calling back.

"Diana, I've been trying to reach you all day. Your workplace said you were in training."

Wait a minute, he tried my workplace? Suddenly, I was unsettled.

"Dan, what is going on?" I inquired, wide-eyed, as I walked to the kitchen to dish up some supper.

"Diana, it isn't good. Kim had a mental breakdown today."

"What? What do you mean? She has been doing so well! What happened? Where is she?" I rapid-fired all these questions without waiting for an answer

"Hang on, Diana, just breathe. Let me tell you what happened."

I took a big deep breath, silencing my voice as my mind exploded with fear.

"Kim wouldn't come to work today. She told us that you and Brent were on your way to the city as she was kicked out of her place for burning a candle."

"What?" I clenched the phone tightly in one hand and the pale grey countertop in the other. "Was she evicted?"

"No. When I couldn't get a hold of her, I grabbed my coat and was going to find her. I was just walking out the door when she called me back—"

"Hadn't you just talked to her?"

"No, she called in and told our secretary that she was not coming in, that she had been evicted and wouldn't be coming back to the program. When I got the message, I immediately sensed something was up, so I tried to call her back. No answer. I tried a few times and then, like I said, I was going to head over to her place when she finally called me back."

"OK, go on," I urged. I wanted to know but didn't at the same time. My body was shaking and Brent looked concerned.

"She told me she was waiting for you and Brent, that she had gotten kicked out and that she wasn't coming back. It took some serious convincing, but we managed to get her to agree to come in to talk with me. Diana, she was a wreck when she got here. She clearly hadn't had any sleep; bags under her eyes, greasy hair, not put together like she normally is."

I quietly listened as my body slid down the white cabinet that had been bearing my weight. Concerned and surprised, Brent crouched down beside me. Full panic set in, and tears welled in my eyes.

"Diana, I had to take her to the hospital. She wasn't making any sense."

My silent tears streamed down my cheeks, and my face flushed as I struggled to breathe. Panicked, I looked towards Brent and motioned for him to get my inhaler. He retrieved it from my blue Roots purse, and I inhaled deeply as Dan continued.

"We got to the Royal University Hospital emergency department around 11:00 a.m. They said we weren't a priority so we sat there for eight hours. I just got home a few minutes ago."

"Where is she?" I asked.

"Diana, she kept saying she was talking to your mom, that her and your mom were walking along the beach with Jesus. She would pick things out of the air and rock back and forth. Diana, I'm sorry, she was admitted to the psychiatric ward of RUH."

The words slammed against my mind as my hand clenched into a fist.

"WHAT?"

"I know, Diana, this comes as a shock to us all. But we did notice some things. Remember that call you had with Anne last week asking about her medical history? Well, that's because we all saw something wasn't right."

I nodded in agreement as if he could see me. Anne, another social worker, asked if Kim had a medical condition that they didn't know about. Of course, I said she did not, but had severe learning issues.

"Remember, she was convinced it was something else?"

"Yeah," I managed to mumble.

"Well, I think she is right. This was an unusual day. I have seen a lot of situations in my day, but nothing quite like this. She kept saying you and Brent were coming to get her, that she was kicked out of her place for performing witchcraft and burning candles, that she scared the baby. When we finally got to see the doctor, they explained she had a psychotic break and admitted her. She is at the Hantelman ward of RUH. You're supposed to meet with the doctors tomorrow morning. Near as I can tell, they have never seen this before."

I recalled the alarm in Anne's voice the previous week and called Dr. Wenzel, Mom's physician for many years in Kerrobert. I didn't know what made me do it other than the unnerving sound of Anne's voice, but I had them fax Mom's file to my office. There was a lot of information, including letters from the neurologist which stated that there was no known name or genetic component that they could figure out. I stopped reading after the first few pages, labelled a few file folders "Mom's health records" and set them on my nightstand. I intended to read more, but information like that knocks me down. I had experienced this illness first hand but had never known much about the medical side of it. I didn't need to read through what happens to the body and mind, I'd seen it.

Dan said I needed to be at RUH by 9:00 the next morning to deal with Kim.

"I'm so sorry, Diana. I know this is incredibly hard. I am here for whatever you need."

"You went above and beyond today, Dan." I mustered. "I am so sorry you couldn't get in touch with me. I can't believe this happened!"

I started sobbing and my body began to shake. I had no idea what I needed to do in the morning, but I knew it was something I had to do alone. I didn't want to stress out my dad, so I figured I shouldn't say anything. And in all honesty, I was ashamed for not seeing what was right in front of me all along. My dad was right, and my foolish twenty-four-year-old mind and ego didn't want to see what age and experience had shown him: something beyond a learning disability was happening here.

Chapter 40

The Long Hall

Pulling into the parking lot at RUH early on Friday, November 6, 2002, the irony of that day being my parents' anniversary is not lost on me. They married in 1971, so today would be their thirty-first anniversary. I silently celebrated the concept of what an anniversary should mean for a happily married couple and was sickened at the thought of what was taken from them and about to be taken from my sister.

I pulled into a tight spot that was right up against a pickup truck and wondered why they had to make these parking lots so darn snug! I slid my car into park, turned off the ignition and grabbed my purse and the files on the seat when I was suddenly overcome with a wave of nausea. I dropped everything, quickly unbuckled myself and opened the door to take in the cool air, hoping it settled this sick feeling stuck in my throat, gagging me. It did. I collected my items again and slipped off of the velvety seat and outside. As I walked to the sliding door of the hospital the nausea took hold again, and I was forced to hunch over and vomit on the snowy cement. Tears slid down my rosy cold cheeks as I collected myself once more. I kept my head down as I rooted in my pocket for a tissue to wipe my mouth and possibly a mint. My body was still shaking as I arrived at the help desk with no idea about where the Hantelman ward was.

"You'll see a long yellow hallway, it's real long," the lady directed me. "At the end you'll enter the ward. Check in with the front desk ladies, and they will tell you where to meet the doctors."

I halfway listened knowing I'd find my way. I'd been going to hospitals my whole life. At the entrance to the long hallway, my legs became heavy, and I struggled to walk. Breathing deeply and clutching the records, I willed my body forward. Thankfully, there was a rail so I clutched it tightly until I got my feet under me again. The nurse wasn't kidding about the length of this hallway; it was going to take forever to walk it at this pace. I was secretly grateful for the length, though, because it gave me time to compose myself.

Strangely enough, I ran into a woman I hadn't seen in years. I heard she went through some challenging things in her life as well. We exchanged hellos, and she said she receives light therapy there, which I know little of, but the sparkle in her eyes told me it was helping, which is great. I'd always had a hard time being mean to people. When the bullies were mistreating others, I tried not to get caught up in it. I probably did some, but I honestly tried to be kind to everyone. She didn't have it easy, and seeing where she has landed emphasized how important being kind to our fellow humans was.

"What are you doing here, Diana?" she asked.

"Um, well, Kim isn't well."

I clutched the files close to my chest and looked at the floor as my eyes welled with the pain I was unable to speak of right then.

She sensed it, moved closer and said, "This place is really good, Diana. She is in good hands here."

Her gentle reassurance surprised me, allowing me to catch my breath and compose myself before I met the doctor. We said goodbye, and I rounded the corner to the common area. The walls were a buttery yellow and the scent was unmistakably "hospital," which pulled me into memories of visiting Mom. I started shaking again, so I grabbed the smooth, long rail that parted the hall from the common area. As I turned my head, I saw a group of people in white coats, ten in all.

"Why are there so many?" I whispered to myself.

As I stepped down the single stair, the team of doctors and nurses stood up, acknowledging me with smiles that I knew masked their confusion. They told me their names, and my mind felt lost as I told them mine. One white coat asked me to sit down and pulled out a chair.

"Diana, we have never seen this before. Kim's behaviour is not typical of our patients," a doctor said.

Before anyone had a chance to weigh in on that comment, I placed the file in the centre of the table.

"I have. This is our mother's file. She has a rare brain atrophy. She was diagnosed when she was twenty-six and I was nine months. Kim needs an MRI. She is on the list, but the letter we got back said it would be a year and a half. That was in September, so we still have a long wait."

It was the first time I'd ever admitted what I should have known all along, and I was somewhat taken aback about what I had just presented. These are doctors, professionals, very smart people, and I just laid out what I believed was the truth.

"Ms. Kirk, what is this illness?" a doctor asked while leafing through the paperwork.

"It doesn't have a name, but one letter to my dad states that none of her children will get it as it's a rare genetic mutation with no family history. My grandma, her mom, was an orphan. She knew her mom, but her dad died young and we don't know how. None of my grandparents' siblings were sick. As far as we know, Mom was the first case. I guess my sister is the second."

As the doctors read through the paperwork, they agreed the MRI needed to happen sooner rather than later.

"We will put her on the cancellation list. Hopefully, she will get one while she stays with us."

As he stated this, questions flew out as my mind turned towards seeing Kim and wondering what to expect.

"How long will she be here? Did you put her on meds? Is she okay now?"

"Yes, we put her on an anti-psychotic medication called Resperidone. When she was seen in emergency, the doctor observed her having full conversations with people who weren't there but also engaging fully with the social worker and staff. She seemed to be following conversations in both worlds. It was like nothing we have seen before. She was agitated and worried that she was going to miss you. It takes a bit for the meds to get into her system to effectively change things, and we will adjust as we see fit. She is also extremely thin; does she have an eating disorder?"

A little annoyed at this blunt question, because it was a sensitive topic for me, I explained that our mother was also rail thin so maybe it's part of the illness. The doctors explained that while she was there they would monitor her food intake to help her gain some.

"We have put her on a supplement called Ensure to encourage weight gain and make sure she is getting proper vitamins. Also, Kim signed herself in here willingly, but you should know that if she chooses to leave, she can unless you have power of attorney to override her decisions. It is something you should look at getting, especially if she isn't well. She needs help and will not be able to make these sorts of decisions alone. She does not have the mental capacity for that."

I nodded in agreement. I had thought of it when speaking with the social worker a few months back, but I was still somewhat shocked that we were at that point. Things seemed to be moving fast and slow all at once, and it was crushing.

"Would you like to visit her now? We can see if she is up," a nurse said as she touched my shoulder gently.

Nervous, and unsure how this was going to go, I stood up and asked the nurse to take me to her. As if reading my mind, the nurse said, "Kim is gentle, not at all angry. She is very agreeable, so don't worry about seeing her. She is your sister, and I know it will do you both good to see each other."

My heart believed this, too, yet the hesitation sat in my anxious soul. Admitting that Kim was sicker than I realized, that she needed to be in a place like this and that I was alone in dealing with it was difficult to take in.

Another nurse brought Kim from her room. She was never a morning person, but it was somehow 10:00 a.m. already which was a good time for her to get up anyway. Kim smiled as she stepped down towards me. I immediately noticed her rigid movements, and it was like the lenses of my glasses suddenly changed from rose-coloured to clear. I could finally see what others said they witnessed. She was clearly sick. Her shuffling feet were another give away that the illness I presented the doctors with was attacking her brain. I wanted to crumble to the floor like I did the night before in the kitchen when I first heard the news, but I knew I had to be strong for her. I steadied myself against the round table as she said hello. Knowing Kim hated hugs, I hesitated before stepping forward and hugging her anyway. As rigid as her body felt, I sensed the softness of her spirit, which has always brought me comfort.

"Can we go to her room now?" I inquired.

"Yes, you can review the medication, and we will continue this discussion after your visit," the nurse said.

As we sat in her room, I was relieved to finally have some time with her. I asked her what happened, but she didn't have answers—no real recollection other telling me she was kicked out of her place for witchcraft, burning candles and scaring the baby. I made a mental note to confirm this with the landlords and find out what was true and what was not. We spent an hour together before I decided to go to her place and figure out what was going on. I remembered I had to go through the list of medications and a few more details with the doctors, so I left her in her room. She was tired and ready for the first nap of her day.

"Do you hear them?" she asked as I was leaving the room. "They're talking to me through the vents!"

"Who is talking to you through the vents?" I asked.

"Them," is all she offered before crawling into bed.

This did not feel like the Kimberley I'd known my whole life. *What happened here?* I asked myself.

Chapter 41

Sorting Out the Messes

The next few weeks was a jumbled mess. Brent and I moved Kim's belongings back to our condo in St. Brieux because, clearly, she could not be alone. The landlords assured us that she was not evicted and verified what we thought: none of these conversations took place. Sadly, this also meant she made it all up, which is yet another indicator something was really wrong.

I had only told Aaron about what happened and where Kim was because Dad would lose it if he found out. Secrets in our family were commonplace; none of us knew he drank, you know! Keeping something from our dad wasn't difficult as we were not very close. Maybe it had something to do with all the things I failed at and had thrown in my face each time we talked. We determined we needed to manage Dad's reactions as well as Kim's, so we chose to deal with one person at a time.

Kim was still in the psych ward in December. Christmas music and decorations were everywhere, but I had yet to do any shopping because my mind was too full of reality. I kept reminding myself, *One foot in front of the other. Just one more step.* We finally got the call to pick Kim up on the afternoon of December 7—after her MRI! That's right, there was a cancellation. The results from the MRI would determine the next steps for Kim, but I could pick her up about 2:30. Excited and scared, I shared the news with Brent and Aaron. Of course, I needed to arrange for more time off, which my workplace had been very understanding about. Our Christmas party was the following week and was the one thing I was actually looking forward to. I enjoyed cutting loose with my co-workers.

I was still full of anxiety as I walked down that long hallway to the Hantelman ward, alone yet again, but I was thankful that I was not vomiting. I reached the nurses' desk and they informed me that the MRI machine was backlogged, so Kim would be another hour. This worked out fine as the doctors wished to speak with me again.

"Kimberley is much calmer now on her medication," the doctor said. "If you are having issues, call the ward and we can assess things over the phone and see if her medications need increasing. She wasn't too happy about having an MRI today; she feels nothing is wrong. Also, I've gone through those records you gave us. May we keep them? Depending on her results, we may need them."

"Uh, sure," I muttered.

We talked for a while longer, the doctor asking more questions about our mother, only some of which I could answer. He wanted to know more about the onset of the illness which was recorded in her medical records. Since our mother was diagnosed December 10, 1978 when I was only nine months old, I was of little help answering what the beginning symptoms were. The doctor was very curious.

"We have set Kim up for an appointment in January with a neurologist," he said. "They should have the results by then and can make a plan from there."

"How long does it take to get the results from an MRI?" I asked.

"Well, that depends. With Christmas coming you probably won't hear before then unless it's bad. Usually takes three to four weeks, which is why we set the neurology appointment for later January, to give ample time for the results to come back."

"Will they call?"

"You may not hear from them until the appointment. They like to share this news in person. The neurologist will examine the results first, and then you and your sister will have an appointment with him to talk about them."

Clearly, we would be waiting longer. Patience is not my strong area. Kim was back in her room when a nurse came to get me.

"She is asking for you. The two of you can pack up her things while I get her medications together."

She led me to the hospital room where I found Kim sitting on her bed, looking out the window.

"I've been waiting for you!" she chided.

We both broke into a smile, happy to be reunited.

"Am I coming home with you?" she asked.

"Of course you are! Brent and I moved all your things back to our place, remember?"

Tilting her head slightly as if trying to find this memory in her mind, she smiled softly and asked, "Do you hear them? They're talking about me again."

Confused and slightly panicked, I inquired, "Who is talking about you? I don't hear anything."

She smiled, turned away and grabbed her duffle bag to begin packing.

"I'll be right back," I assured her and quickly left the room.

I pulled a nurse aside and said, "She isn't better! She is fooling you! She just asked me if I could hear people in the vents again!"

My voice was full of panic—I was terrified! The nurse patted my arm and assured me Kim was going to be OK.

"This is her new normal and she seems content," the nurse said. "If you need anything during the weekend, here is our number. Just call and someone will help. We are still working on her medications, so if she needs a higher dose, we can authorize over the phone or move up her medication times. You two will be okay."

Again, it felt like everything was slow and fast all at once in my world. The weeks she was in there were slow and now everything was moving far too quickly. I couldn't tell them I was scared or not ready. Like most of our lives, we were not afforded the luxury of choice but rather the obligation of duty.

Kim was standing beside me, smiling and ready to go. Her expression said she didn't sense my apprehension, and I was relieved. We were on our way back home to an uncertain future.

Kim was happy to see that she now got our upstairs bedroom. We moved our office to the basement and gave her the room beside ours so we could keep a closer eye on her. Her things were all set up as she liked, tidy and in order, and we planned on picking up our Christmas tree in Cudworth the next day and decorating it. Kim's eyes lit up with the wonder of a child when we shared the news with her.

Chapter 42

Ghosties

It didn't take long for Kim's ghosties (her term for her psychosis) to appear. The first thing we noticed came in conversations, but not with us. In her bedroom with her door closed, Kim had full on conversations with herself. I could hear talking, but the cordless phone was in its place. Baffled, I slowly opened the door to her room and found her in the corner on the floor having a full conversation with someone who wasn't visible to me, so I hastily closed the door.

My heart was racing as I fumbled through my purse to find the number of the psych ward. Brent had gone to find a Christmas tree. My body, full of tingles, struggled to hold me up as I dialed the emergency number, hoping for help on the other end. A nurse picked up on the third ring, and I explained what was happening.

"Oh yes, she was just released yesterday I see," the nurse said after getting Kim's chart. "Feel free to move her evening dose up, that should help."

All I could think of was that I was not capable of dealing with this. I wished they had listened to me when I told them she wasn't ready to leave and that I knew this was going to happen! I was angry that our life now was trying to get the right dosage at the correct time of day to keep her ghosties away. I felt like a failure and a fool. I failed to keep Kim safe, and I was a fool to think I could help. I was at a loss for how to help, and I had no idea what the hell I was dealing with. I was in way over my head.

I popped my head into Kim's room and told her it was time for her medication. I interrupted her ghostie time, but she didn't seem flustered. Happily and almost indifferent to what was going on, she followed me to the kitchen where I had set out her the pills and a glass of water. She dutifully took them while I prayed for them to kick in fast. They worked for a while, then we were back to the same situation, so I called to get approval to administer more medication. By the time Sunday rolled around we had changed her med dosage three times, and I was mentally exhausted. Kim came out of her bedroom looking like she hadn't slept and asked if we could decorate the Christmas tree. Stringing blue lights over the fresh pine Brent brought from Big Way was a good distraction. We laughed while reminiscing about the ugly tree Brent and I first brought home in the back seat of my car a couple of years before. It was full and lush, but only at the bottom. The branches were sparce part-way up, making it look more like a pear than a tree! It was hilarious. As the laughter encompassed our bodies, I felt relief for the first time since picking Kim up.

Brent got up early that Monday morning as he worked at 6:30. My job didn't start until 8:00, but something told me I wouldn't be able to leave Kim alone for very long. I heard Brent get out of our bed, leave our room and come back quickly.

"Diana, it's Kim. You'd better come."

I ripped myself from the comfortable warmth of our bed, the sense of peacefulness I carried to bed after decorating the tree replaced by the familiar feeling of anxiety and panic. I put my high prescription glasses on and rushed down the hall and into Kimberley's bedroom and a shocking scene. She was pulling her hair out, smashing her fists against her legs and mumbling "No!" Brent needed to leave for work, so we were unsure what to do. Brent couldn't be late because there were still bills to pay—we still needed to work. I brought Kim her medication, but she was frantic with fear.

"What's going on, Sweetie?" I asked quietly.

"There are snakes everywhere! They are coming out of my hair! The ghosties are trying to stuff me into a mattress and I don't want to go!"

I held her face lovingly and looked directly in her eyes.

"You are safe, Kim," I said gently. "We're at home. I'm your sister, and these pills will help."

The look of fear in her eyes sent chills down my spine. Her eyes were bloodshot, her face stained with tears, and I wondered how long the terror had had a grip over her. We breathed in and out slowly. I don't know where this idea came from, but all I had was instinct to navigate this nightmare.

After several minutes she was calm enough to take her medication. It was 7:00 a.m., and I had to get ready for work, but I knew she couldn't be alone. I sat on the bed and gently stroked her hair as her heavy eyes closed. I waited until she was asleep, another half hour, before I left her side and devised my plan.

In the bathroom, I washed my face and brushed my teeth. The mirror captured my attention after I put my contacts in; I looked like absolute shit, but I did not care. Kim was fast asleep as I slipped out, but who knew for how long? I had to make this quick. As I walked into the office, people's words chased my ears, but I paid no attention. I had to talk with my boss and call my doctor in Melfort. The three days with Kim had not gone well. We needed a plan.

Larry, my boss, was compassionate and understanding, as I knew he would be. Grateful, I called the clinic from my cubicle. I didn't want Kim to hear the call because it might wake her up—or worse—send her over the edge. Hell, this whole shitshow was sending me over the edge, but I had no options. I could not run away. It's not how I'm built.

I was grateful to hear that I should bring Kimberley in ASAP. The panic and urgency with which I pleaded must have helped. I'd gotten the time off, I'd contacted the doctor, and now I had to get Kim out of bed. She was still fast asleep, so I decided to let her rest until lunch since she didn't get any sleep. In the meantime, I called Aaron to give him an update, and he told me he would come if I needed him to.

Rousing Kim from her slumber wasn't easy, but she was cooperative as I gave her more medication (as the psych ward suggested). Twenty-five minutes later we're in Melfort where we started this several months ago. I asked the nurse if I could see the doctor alone first. The nurse was happy to comply, but I warned her of what may happen without me there. She assured me that Kimberley would be okay for a few minutes, but she would get the doctor if she wasn't. When I was called, Kim seemed content to stay where she was. She didn't know we were there for her. Mind you, she didn't know much that made sense at that time. My sister wasn't there, only her body was.

Debriefing Dr. Wind was difficult. I was in tears, an absolute mess. This was the first time I'd allowed myself to feel the weight of what was going on. I didn't want to scare Kim with my fears, so I hid them as best I could at home. The doctor was empathetic to our situation and told me he was going to make some calls to get the results from the MRI. He also said these usually took a few weeks to come back, so there was a good chance we wouldn't hear for a while.

I held Kim's hand as she sat down, the nurse had brought her to join me in the outpatient room. He asked her a series of questions about the previous few weeks, and some of the answers made sense while others did not. He asked her if it was okay to call for her MRI results, and she agreed.

Chapter 43

Dark

As Kim and I sit side by side holding hands, Dr. Wind walked in and I instantly knew what he was going to say. It was written all over his face.

"I have the results," he said.

I flashed back to RUH doctor's words on Friday, and I knew this wasn't good: "If the results are in quickly, there is a good chance they aren't going to be good. So if you don't hear from us, that's a good thing."

My heart quickened and I broke out into a full-body sweat. *Deep breaths*, I told myself as I clutched Kim's hand tighter. She looked over at me, as I was unable to hide my emotions.

"I'm afraid this isn't the news we were hoping for. Kim, your brain appears to be shrinking. There is some sort of atrophy happening. In comparing against your mom's scans, it would seem you have whatever illness she has. I am so sorry."

Coming to sit in front of us, his eyes caught mine as the magnitude of his words puzzled my mind. Kim, surprisingly quicker to process this, seemed OK. Perhaps it was the medication or maybe she had known all along.

"I am so sorry, Kimberley and Diana. I had hoped to have better news," he said as he grabbed our hands. There was a softness in this gesture that I was not ready for. Pity. "I am going to leave you here for a while to process before we make a plan. Take as much time as you need."

I began gasping for air, so I reached into my pocket for my Ventolin inhaler. This was just too much; I could not comprehend the weight of the diagnosis. Unable to hide my pain any longer, I broke down in heaping sobs of grief. Kim quietly cried. We held each other tight, and I vowed to find a way through this with her.

"You are not alone, Kim. I will fight this with you," I said through my tears.

I knew that once we left the office, we needed to face our loved ones and share this news. If we stayed there, I felt like we could hide from the world. I knew each step from now on, just as it had always been, was going to be difficult. I would have to do things, make decisions, deal with people. I'd have to handle Dad, the doctors, the appointments. Once I left the safety of these walls, life as we know knew it would change profoundly. I was wondering what the doctor was going to suggest we do next.

As he stepped back into our private room of hell, the doctor said, "Diana, can I have a word with you? Kimberley, the nurse is here to check your vitals. Is it okay if I talk to your sister?"

Kim, being her agreeable self, nodded while I followed the doctor to the room across the hall.

"I felt this conversation is best between us, Diana, as you are Kim's primary caregiver."

Caregiver. I touched my lips as I whispered the word to myself. I didn't like the feeling of that.

"I'm not ready to be a caregiver, Dr. Wind! I am barely able to take care of myself!" I said, shaking my hands as if trying to rid myself of the role.

I was uncomfortable and anxious. I didn't feel in place. In fact, I felt like I was whirling in a tornado, being flung about with no control.

"We feel it's best to admit Kim for a few days because we don't know if she could become suicidal at this news," the doctor said, snapping me back to reality.

Because of Kim's deep faith in God, I hadn't even considered this an option for her—me perhaps, but not her!

"Diana, you need time to process this. It's a lot for anyone, but you're twenty-four; you need to line up some support for you both. Let us take care of her for now so you can process this."

"OK," I said, looking at the calendar. "Dr. Wind, is it really December 10?"

"Yes, it is. I know this news just before Christmas is simply awful."

"It is, but did you know that our mother got the same news my sister received today on December 10, 1978?"

We were silent for a moment while we let the irony wash over us. I was at a total loss.

"I know where this battle takes us; I've lived this already," I said. "How am I going to tell our family? What am I going to do?"

I sputtered out questions knowing there were no answers, just actions that must be taken.

"I'm so sorry, Diana. I can't imagine how this must feel."

I signed the papers to admit Kimberley to the hospital and said, "We have to go home to get her some things. She will want her teddy bear and some pajamas."

"No problem. We can finish the rest of the paperwork at the hospital," he said. "We are going to keep her medicated so she can sleep; she looks like she needs it."

Kim was sitting in her room with the nurse looking at a children's picture book and talking about art, which reminded me that sometimes we find authentic kindness in strangers. I was in tears once again as I sat down next to them. Dr. Wind explained the plan to her while I grabbed her hand again. Kim looked to me for reassurance.

"It's OK, Kim, this way you'll get some sleep," I said with a smile. "We both know you need that."

She nodded and was happy to hear we would go back to our place to pick up a few of her things. The doctor and his nurse hugged us both, and we walked through the waiting room full of patients. Strangers' eyes looked at us with what I can only describe as sadness.

Some smiled, but when they met my eyes, the ache of my soul sent sadness to theirs, and it showed.

Our drive back to St. Brieux was quiet as our minds tried to catch up to our ears.

"Diana, you know what? This is OK! Now I know I am not crazy, that something is wrong with me and that I'm not stupid!"

She was relieved and felt comforted knowing she was not completely going insane and that there was a reason for her illness. I turned my face away as the tears welled up again. I had never thought that this could be relief for her.

"Diana, we have to tell Brent when we are home. That is going to be hard."

I swallowed deeply, knowing she was right. Brent, our dad, our brothers, friends, aunts, uncles, cousins, co-workers—I would have to tell them all.

"Brent is going to be good about it, Kim. We will sort things out."

Deep down I knew most of this would fall to me, but I liked the idea of sharing the load. I knew the first person who would offer help would be Aaron.

Brent was already home from work, and Kim and I anxiously shared a glance as we walk into the condo together. Brent, coming from the bedroom, greeted us, and he knew by the look on our faces that we had bad news.

"I'm sick," Kim said. "Mom's illness. I'm going to stay in the hospital for a few days so I can get sleep and maybe the ghosties won't bother me there."

Deep down Brent knew Kim was sick. He had shared with me before that there was more wrong than a learning disability. Today, however, Brent was in shock. We all hugged and cried. Our world was collapsing in front of us, and I could not keep it together.

"We are going to pack up some things and I'll take her in," I said.

"Can you come with us, Brent?" Kim quietly requested.

He nodded as we went to her bedroom to pack a few things in the duffle bag that we had just unpacked on Friday.

Kim was surprisingly chatty in the back seat on the drive back to Melfort. Stuffed animal in hand, she asked me how I would handle telling Dad. We both knew this news would send him into a rage then into a depression he may not be able to come back from.

"At first, I wasn't sure," I said as I turned around to face her. "But then I decided Aaron will tell him. He should hear it in person."

"Good idea," Kim said.

What I didn't say was how I planned to tell Aaron. My bargaining chip was that I had to be in the room to hear this news with Kim, so he could be in the room when he told our father. It would be just like when there were things to be done as children, good or bad; we dug in and did them together.

We had answers and would be faced with life-altering choices, and this reality caught up with me as we walked into the hospital, so I made a quick break for the bathroom across the hall, slammed the door and let the solitude wash over me for a few moments. *Breathe, just breathe,* I told myself as if talking myself off of a cliff. Brent tried to come in, but I told him I needed a minute. I was falling apart. Checking Kim in was quite easy since the majority of the paperwork was completed at the clinic earlier. Clearly, the staff had been briefed on what we were handling, and they were extra compassionate. As if treating Kimberley with the fragility of a small child, they led her to her room with promise of pudding and movies.

"We will bring a TV in," the nurse said, "and you can enjoy a show or sleep as much as you wish. No need to get up early; you just enjoy yourself."

Even though Kim was mentally unstable and her brain was literally shrinking, I was comfortable that she was in capable hands. They were administering a sleeping pill shortly which would calm her enough for sleep. Between that and the anti-psychotic, a combination the doctors agreed upon, would make her stay go relatively smoothly. Patting my arm and catching my eye, a nurse took me aside as we walked behind the others.

"Here, have a rest," she said as she led us to a small, quiet room to sit awhile. "You have had quite the day, young lady."

I tried to push back the tears and keep my composure. I nodded.

"If you need anything, you know we are here for you too. I hear your mom has the same illness. This must be so hard."

At that, all my composure left and the emotion surged through my veins, replacing my anxiety. I welcomed the release. The nurse held my hand while handing me a tissue.

"I know you have to be strong for your sister, but you also need to be taken care of. What you are going through is enormous for any of us, but you are young; you need support too."

I assured her I had good friends and some family. I was tired, but went to Kim's room to see that she was settling in. She was getting sleepy from the medication, so she was lying on her bed, stuffy still in hand. The darkness of winter was lit by the streetlights shining against the snow. I noticed it had started to snow again and realized we had to get home so I could make some calls. Kim was asleep with an expression of contentment on her face. She was certainly much more peaceful than I was once she heard what was happening. She was so hard on herself for things she could not control. I glanced outside again, mesmerized by the falling snow.

I gently kissed my sister's forehead, a gesture she would never allow if she were awake. She felt warm and smelled of baby powder. That scent from her deodorant annoyed me for years because I found it too babyish for a grown woman, but now I found comfort in the softness.

"Whatever makes you happy," I whispered before leaving her side. "I will be back tomorrow after I get some sleep and make some calls."

I'd already called my office since they needed to know if I was coming in. Thankfully, they were a good workplace and gave me some flex time. If I felt like coming in, for support or a distraction, I could, but if I didn't, they wouldn't force it. I had been assured that I would get a few days of paid leave so I could still afford food and rent. The last thing they wanted to do was add any financial burden, and I was deeply grateful to them. As we walked to my car, tears fell as soft as the snow on my cheeks. We were silent on the drive home, both lost in our thoughts. The feeling of being in over my head was back, and I knew I had to call Aaron and Chris to get some help.

Brent rustled up some food at home, but I wasn't interested. Hunger had been replaced by deep pain and grief. After exchanging hugs and some tears, I picked up the phone to make a call I both wanted to and didn't want to make. I wanted to make it because I knew I would be supported; they would come and try their level best to share the burden of this pain. I didn't want to make the call because telling others made it more real.

Aaron was shocked. Like me, he knew something wasn't right, but none of us wanted to see exactly what it was.

"Did you tell Dad?" he inquired.

I grew quiet at the thought of what I had to ask him.

"Diana, I know this has been a hard day, but we have to tell Dad," he said, stating the obvious.

Somehow, he always knew what I was thinking with a pause in conversation. I took the deepest breath of the day and said, "I know. But here's the thing, I had to sit with Kim and deal with the news, I had to make an immediate plan with the doctors, and I had to carry the weight of all of this squarely on my shoulders. I don't think I can handle telling Dad on my own. You know how he yells and freaks out. A conversation like this cannot be had over the phone, Aaron; it should be done in person. I can't come to Plenty and tell him because I need to remain close to Kim…"

Thankfully, I didn't have to continue. Aaron caught my drift instantly and replied, "You want me to tell him? OK, I can do that. He will be upset, in person or over the phone, but you're right, it has to be done in person."

I broke down again. I'd never been good at asking for anything because I was usually chided for it. I'm much better at giving than receiving, at hiding than being transparent. The stress, the chaos, the diagnosis all flooded in as I gasped for air. Instinctively, I knew the tears needed to wash over me. Crying was a sign of weakness in my family, yet when I released my tears, it felt very natural. Since it conjured up much stress for my dad to see me cry, I mostly allowed the tears in solitude, but I was deeply grieving and succumbing to the weight of the days, the weeks and the months. As I stopped for a moment to find a tissue, I heard the familiar crack in Aaron's voice as he tried to console me. We were both broken, both trying to put each other's pieces back together. It was a moment of release, of fear, of knowing and not knowing. The mixture left us vulnerable, yet we knew one thing for certain: we supported each other. With that, I let the tears come. As they cascaded down my cheeks, my chest tightened, and that familiar feeling of not being able to breathe crept up.

"After I talk with Dad, I'll come up, okay? Diana? Just breathe. We are going to get through this," Aaron reassured me as I sobbed.

I knew little would comfort me, but a small part of me felt gratitude that he would be coming to see us. I searched my bedside table for my inhaler. I just needed to breathe. I found it and pulled the phone receiver down from my mouth and inhaled my medicine. *Just breathe, Diana.* I felt my lungs open up. Sweet relief.

Still on the phone, I shuffled to Kim's bed to seek comfort as I had done since I was a child. The only problem was, she was not there. I wanted to be next to her, to lay beside her as we had as small girls going through fearful moments like this together. The awareness of her empty room left me wrestling with my thoughts. *Why Kim? Why not me?* I made eye contact with Brent in the hallway. He looked haggard, and I quietly thought to myself, *He didn't sign up for this.*

"We could take Kim out for the day, go Christmas shopping somewhere!" Aaron continued. "How is Prince Albert? Should we do that? I'm in the market for one of those coffee tables that lifts up so it's like TV tray height, you know? They're cool!"

Aaron always found a way to soothe my soul. I quieted down some as we planned a day to Christmas shop. Kim and I hadn't planned on coming home for Christmas this year, but it seemed fitting that we did. We had to see Dad sooner or later. He would be a mess. We both knew that once he heard the news, a tailspin of drinking would continue because this would be yet another reason not to stop.

"We should be there to support Dad," I suggested.

"Yeah, but after we get you and Kim stable. Dad will have his friends come, and that's what his sister is there for. She will help. We need to get some things sorted out before we can support him. Priorities. Remember, Diana, Kim is first on the list. She needs the most of our help right now, OK? You got this. You've done such a good job with her over the years. This comes as a shock to us all, but it doesn't undo all the good that you were able to give her this year. She broke free from her shell, you got her out in the world, found a place for her to live. You managed to get funding and a place for her to work. You did so much—"

"Yeah, but for what? We ended up in a shittier place than before! This is a God damn nightmare, and we are the stars of the show! And the worst part is, we know her future!" I let all the pain flood out. "We know where this ends up, Aaron, and it's not in a good place!" My words were full of panic, which sent Brent rushing into Kim's bedroom where I was huddled up under her covers.

"I know," Aaron said as he began to cry too.

There was not much left to say other than to finalize a plan for his arrival.

"I have to call Chris now. When are you telling Dad?"

"I will tell Dad first thing tomorrow, then come up later afternoon to see you."

We hoped Chris could stay with Dad while we handled things with Kim. I almost forgot that this was a Monday and most of us should have been at our regular jobs. So much had happened over the past month, and the days seemed to blend together.

"I have to make some calls and juggle some things," he said. "If I can't make it tomorrow, Wednesday for sure. Will you be okay until then?"

I assured him I would and agree to make the rest of the calls in the morning after some sleep.

Brent had drawn me a bath and offered again to heat up supper. "Diana, you have to eat."

I was not hungry, so I declined as nicely as I could. I knew he was just trying to help. I did take him up on the bath though. When I leaned back in the tub, I let the water wash over my head. Where the tears ended and the water began, I'm not sure, but the warmth of the water enveloped my nakedness washing away my tears. The lavender bath salts calmed me enough that I was ready for sleep. There were many more calls to make in the morning, but Aaron was right, tomorrow would be there. I couldn't get the haunting thoughts of Kim's future out of my mind or the question *Why is it that Kim and Mom are both ill, yet I didn't get this mysterious disease? Why them? Why not me?*

I crawled into bed next to Brent, and he held me as I continued to weep tears that contained all the hopes and dreams I had for a bright future for my sister. I knew the light of hope was slowly diming, but now I saw nothing, just darkness.

Chapter 44

Blur

Over the course of the next few days, I framed up a support structure for Kim. My first call on Tuesday morning was to my other brother, who wasn't as surprised as Aaron and I.

"I knew something was wrong with her for a while, Diana, but I didn't have the heart to tell you," he said. "This is awful. I wish I could come down, but I don't have days off until Christmas."

Chris and I hadn't been overly close over the previous few years, which might have been due to us both being opinionated and alike in some ways. Chris worked in the Alberta oil industry, so days off were few and far between. The offset was the money; it was good, but it came with the price tag of time. There went my hope of having him help Dad through this for a few days until we could make it back home.

"Have you told Dad yet?" he asked.

"Aaron should be at the farm now," I said.

"What are you going to do now? Like, what's the plan or the next step?"

Chris knew just as much as the rest of us that planning didn't mean a plan to cure Kimberley. The plan he referred to was how to handle the full time caregiving and financial burden this disease commanded. This was a question I was asked many times over the next few days, weeks and years, and the answer was always the same:

"One foot in front of the other. I can't run, I won't. Honestly, I don't know." Chris understood what I meant, and he trusted we would find answers as we went along. He decided he would call Dad after we got off the phone. This was news no parent wanted to hear, and Chris was a parent, so he could relate to Dad more than Aaron and I.

"Thank you, Chris, for being there for Dad, and us. I'll keep in touch with how things are going," I reassured.

"Yeah, no problem. It's what brother is for, Diana. We are in this together. I know this is hard. Like I said, I have work, otherwise I'd be there. I'll be home for Christmas with Breanna. I get it off," he said.

His thoughts echoed mine: I was hoping Breanna would be out for a visit. She was the sunshine and hope we all needed. We hung up. One call down, and what felt like a million others to go.

I circled back to Aaron to find out how Dad took it.

"Not well," Aaron said. "He kept saying 'Oh God' and holding his face. It was awful. But it's done now. How did it go with Chris?"

I figured that was exactly how the conversation with Dad went, and it dawned on me that I needed to call Dad to explain how I failed yet again.

"Chris was OK and was going to call Dad. He can't get time off work, but he and B will be home for Christmas."

Aaron was happy to hear we would all be together.

"What are your plans?" I inquired.

"When do you think Kim will be out? Maybe I can come Friday? Just thinking out loud here. With work and Dad and Chris not able to get time off, I should probably be around for him. Or what do you think?"

Aaron rambled until I cut him off.

"I am totally OK with having a bit of time to wrap my head around this while Kim is in the hospital. It would be better to have you here once she's out. I have Brent here, and Lindsay is coming out this afternoon. Some other friends will be here throughout the week, so we will be taken care of. I've got a Christmas party Saturday that I really don't want to miss. I know that sounds strange, but I think it might be a good time to cut loose. How about you come Thursday evening, then we go pick up Kim together Friday? The doctor said she would be staying five or so days. You can stay with her Saturday night when Brent and I are out."

With that plan hatched, Dad would have Aaron for a couple days before he came up here to help me tackle the caregiving.

After I hung up the phone, I felt relieved. Lindsay would be there around 2:30 and stay for supper, which she planned to bring, and a sleepover. She was a lifelong friend who walked alongside me no matter what difficulty the world tossed my way. She was my comfort; my best friend.

When I told Auntie Betty, I knew she was devastated, but emotions didn't surface easily for her. It was a hard call to make since she had always stepped up to be a mother figure in our lives. She loved us a lot, and to share this news with her was just about as hard as sitting in that room with Kim. She was five and a half hours away, and it was just before Christmas so she wouldn't be coming down. Secretly, this hurt me deeply because I wanted to feel a hug from her. If I had asked her, maybe she would have, but I would never know.

"I am only a phone call away, Diana, at any time. You just call and I'll answer," she said.

Auntie had truly always been there from the time we were little, and she played a valuable role in shaping us. For people I loved deeply, I made concessions and knew she was with me in spirit.

Chapter 45

Christmas Shopping

Christmas lights were strung on the stores and carols played on repeat as Aaron and I took Kimberley shopping on Saturday. We had planned for Friday, but she didn't get released until midday and was still relatively groggy although content. She had been substantially more settled since the diagnosis, and I'm sure the sleep aids helped as well. She had struggled with insomnia for years, so this was the most rested she had been in a while. I sensed having some answers, no matter how devastating, was far less painful than countless thoughts of self-blame and belittling. She came to terms with something she perhaps knew all along, and it somehow made it easier even though she was the one going through it. It was a paradox, but it also gave us some reprieve from the intensity of our feelings.

As I walked into the mall, I realized this was Kim's first time out in public for quite some time. It felt normal and nice to do something "fun." Her eyes brimmed with joy, which matched her smile. Time with us to enjoy something normal for a change was a gift, and we all knew it. I immediately wondered if we would get to do this again, but I caught myself and pushed those fears and feelings far down before I turned into a blubbering mess. The plan was to have a good day!

Kim loved looking at all the pretty decorations. We walked down memory lane in Zellers as it was the only store besides the SAAN store that we got clothing when we were kids. Oh wait, every once in a while Peavey Mart carried winter underwear for kids! We giggled at all the things Dad would get at that. The laughter made us all feel better in such a tough time.

Aaron wandered off in The Brick to look for this coffee table; he was a man on a mission. Kim and I did what we'd always done and enjoyed daydreaming about pieces of furniture we could have in our dream homes. Creating and daydreaming had always been a joy to do together. We didn't have much growing up, but we had an imagination, and that continually entertained us. From art to pretending, creating was what our minds and souls did to pass the time and bring us joy.

We were happy to window shop and weigh in on Aaron's coffee table decision; it was all we needed at that moment. After a while, Kim and I wandered back into Zellers, which was just to the left of The Brick. Kim was determined to get me a Christmas gift even though she didn't have much. Finding nothing, we went the other way down the mall, towards Sears. Kim stopped at the bookstore, asked me who my favourite author was and then told me to show her. I picked Maya Angelou. She was wise with a heart song worth its weight in gold, Maya could string words together like an astute pianist could play my favourite song. We browsed the aisles and finally found the red hard cover called *Wouldn't Take Nothing for My Journey*. Aaron gently told me to go to another section, so I did. He helped her with her surprise for me, which was a sweet and endearing gesture.

We stopped at Canadian Tire and the A&W drive thru before we headed back to St. Brieux. Aaron stayed with Kim while Brent and I went out to my Christmas party for work. It was only a few days before Christmas; Kim, Brent and I would be going to the farm for it, and it would be the first time we would all be together in several years. I was looking forward to the visit. Kim seemed less hesitant about going home and seeing our dad as well. When she initially left several months before, Kim was running away, just like I had. Now it was time to go back home and reconcile her past with her bleak future. There was no more time to hold grudges against our father; it was time to forgive.

Chapter 46

Home for the Holidays

Freshly fallen snow covered the driveway to the farm as we pulled into the yard in Brent's green Grand Am. Chris had called a couple days before to tell us about Dad's new girlfriend.

"He seems pretty happy with her; she is helping him deal with what's going on with Kim. I think she's good for him!"

I was relieved there would be someone other than just us kids, and she might be a good buffer between Dad and me. I was also hopeful that since he is dating, he would be sober and wouldn't pick fights or pit Chris and me against each other. He enjoyed stirring the shit pot, but you know what they say: "Those who stir the shit pot have to lick the spoon!"

My childhood lay in front of me as I walked into our farmhouse, and I was met with the savoury aroma of a roasted turkey and all the fixings. This was the first time in many years I was not the one making the meal. Dee, my sister-in-law, and I usually took turns hosting. This year, however, Dad's new lady friend made us the feast! *Good first impression*, I thought. Slipping off our boots, Kim and I hollered that we were home! No quicker was Kim's voice past her lips than a little puppy buzzed past me, almost knocking me off balance as I removed my second shoe.

"GIZMO!" Kim screamed.

He was shaking with an excitement I have never seen from an animal as Kim sat down with this little Shih Tzu. The moment was beautiful, and the love permeated from each of them like kindred spirits reunited. It was truly a wondrous Christmas miracle!

I was distracted by the puppy and didn't see the lady in the kitchen near the entrance, so Brent nudged me and I looked up. I was met with a skintight velvet dress and barely contained breasts! This was our father's new girlfriend, Trudy. I did my best to keep my eyes focused on her face and not farther south, but it was difficult since it was quite the show down there. She clearly did not understand the rules in this house; we were a fairly modest bunch. Her memo must have gotten lost. Dad was on her heals, clearing his throat, which signalled his discomfort.

"I see why your dad is so happy!" Brent whispered with a wink.

Dad, who hadn't seen any of us since the diagnosis, greeted Kim first; she remained on the floor cuddling the puppy, but looked up and awkwardly smiled.

"He sure missed you!" he said.

Nothing was mentioned to her about the illness. Avoidance was the default setting we all used in uncomfortable or awkward situations.

"This is my friend, Trudy," he said, as he looked towards me for approval.

Remember, I was the mother of this household, Aaron, the father, and our father, the child. Odd, I know, but the dynamics were laid out many years ago, and him bringing this lady into the mix did not change these roles or unspoken rules.

"Supper smells great," I said, easing the awkwardness.

"Thanks!" Trudy and Dad both replied.

We went into the dining room/living room, and I noticed the house was very tidy and they'd put up our old Christmas tree! It was sparsely decorated, and I reached out to touch one of our old Christmas balls that was made out of a burnt out outdoor Christmas light. *It's surprising what stands the test of time*, I thought.

Kim took her suitcase to her room to unpack, which left the four of us together.

"Kim looks good; she has gained weight," Dad commented.

"Yes, she is on Ensure, you know, the stuff Grandma used to be on—"

"I knew she was sick, Diana. I knew something was wrong. You tried to make her independent, to make her like you! You thought I was doing a terrible job by keeping her here, but I knew it!"

Dad's voice was raised, and I cowered at his yell. I wanted to hang my head in shame and stand up to him all at once; this was the battle I'd never win, so I had to choose wisely: Should I engage? Strangely, I now understood I had a choice, which was something I was not afforded when I lived under this roof. But I had grown, and even though Dad's words could try to bring me down, I didn't have to stoop if I didn't want to.

"Les, dear, calm down. I am sure this hasn't been easy on any of you. Starting an argument about who was right isn't going to change things," said Trudy.

This surprised me. I didn't know Trudy, but I was beginning to like her.

Dad shot me a "we're not finished" look and went quiet. *More unusual behaviour.* I decided to defend myself, but not raise my voice.

"Dad, Kim is sick, and it doesn't matter who knew when; we know now. We have lots of things to figure out. This has been incredibly hard for us, so let's get through Christmas and try to make the best of it—"

A noise of the door and a sweet little voice chiming in amongst my brothers interrupted me.

"Breanna is here!" I yelled as I launched up from my chair.

Breanna is Chris's daughter and is the sweetest little six-year-old you have ever met. She has hazel eyes and long brown hair; she is the spitting image of Chris. I picked up Breanna in a loving embrace and helped her unzip her snowsuit. We were not much of a hugging family, but this year it seemed fitting. Breaking free from Breanna for a moment, I embraced both my brothers. Chris, always trying to be cool, broke into a smile, but I saw the sadness that has captured us all. I hollered for Kim. Gizmo led the way down the narrow wooden staircase, the same staircase I fell down during a power outage many moons ago. Aaron told Kim that Gizmo hadn't been the same since she left nine months before, which made her smile.

"What do you think of Dad's new lady friend?" Chris asked.

"She seems alright," I mused.

Kim shocked us all by saying what had been on our minds: "Chris, I'm sick."

"Yeah, I heard. That sucks," Chris replied.

Everyone was silent but thinking the same thing: *How did I escape this disease?*

Chapter 47

Hope Floats

I gasped as I stood at our mother's bedside; I was overwhelmed and panicked but tried to hold it together. Everyone but Dad came for the day we dreaded: visiting our mother for the first time since Kim's diagnosis. Chris brought Breanna, who is a source of light and hope for everyone, and she added so much joy with just her smile. Her tiny hand would find mine and together we would stand in the quiet. Her imagination shared little memories or anecdotes that were both necessary and well-timed on a day like today.

Aaron, Deanne, Brent and I had the hardest time not breaking down. Moments of torture were eased with other moments of endearing understanding and B's smiles. No words had crossed our mother's lips in about two decades, so listening to our own voices make one-sided conversation with Mom was somewhat of a skill set. Her words were locked away, so we listened with our souls. *Soon*, I thought, *this is the only way I will be able to communicate with Kim*. With that thought, I raced into the hallway where Aaron, Deanne and Brent were wiping away their tears. An acquaintance once said, "At least Kim doesn't have any kids, so they won't be losing their mother," and the thought sickens and comforts me. I was sick knowing that Kim always wanted to be a mom, and I knew she would be a far better one than I because she was more patient and had a gentle nature. I was a ram, pushing my way through life. Kim was soft,

I was hard. Puzzled at that thought, I began to understand that we both possessed those traits depending on what we were dealing with. The selfish part of me wanted to have a piece of her to hold onto and love in the form of her child, but the other part sided with the acquaintance. Indeed, I would not wish losing your mother to a horrific illness such as this on any child.

My thought process was broken at the sound of someone blowing their nose. I looked up through my teary eyes and saw Aaron, red-eyed and visibly upset. I reached to console him. Only the children of our mother truly knew how this illness robbed you of your functioning body, locking away your voice and mind and throwing away the key. Only mother's children knew the heaviness which each of us carried in the form of survivor's guilt that it is not us. How, like a spinning roulette wheel, the marble didn't land on my name. As if reading my thoughts, Aaron said, "We should go back in there."

"We should" I agreed.

I walked across the hall into the room, and Chris and Kimberley watched us enter. Kim was stone-faced, and Chris held Breanna while he told stories to Mom. I made it back to my post beside Mom's bed and grabbed the bedside rail which was always in an upright position in case she rolled out. This was ironic as she could not go anywhere; she could not command her body to willfully move. In any case, I was grateful for the rail, especially after the bomb Kim dropped as we all kept vigil around the bed.

"I understand, Mom. I know what you're going through. I'm sick too. I am just like you. Everyone always said that and now it's true," she said while she gently rubbed our mother's slender, milky white hand.

My knees buckled as the words shattered my heart. Desperate to gain composure, I let out a large gasp and gripped the rail tighter, careful to avoid eye contact. The room was filled with sobs as both Brent and Deanne left. I could not. My feet felt glued to the shiny white tile floor as I struggled for breath. My eyes met Kim's. Tears had broken free from me and raced each other down my cheeks. Kim stood, emotionless. *It is haunting,* I thought, *how could she move from open to closed? Kim had always been steady until she was not.*

Chris decided to do what he does best: make us giggle. This had been his role since we were small children visiting Mom in the hospital.

"Nurse! Nurse," yelled a random patient who had been wandering the halls for a few minutes.

We heard her before, but this time, in the thick of our silence, her voice asked us to be more attentive.

"Yes, I'll be there is a minute!" Chris responded.

The rollercoaster ride of emotions shot us back up to the throes of a good belly laugh, which was just what we all needed. Tears of pain turned to tears of joy.

I turned to my right to see a lady standing amongst us. She stood tall even though she was shorter than I. Her hair was short and silvery, and she tossed her fingers hastily through it, toque in hand.

"Well, hello there, Margie! How are you doing?" she said as if we were not there. She didn't break eye contact with our mother. "I see you have your children here today, on Christmas! What a wonderful treat for you!"

My mind tried to catch up to my eyes. *Who is this? When did she get here? How did I not hear her come in?* She squeezed her way between Aaron and I without so much as a pardon me and continued the one-sided conversation.

"I won't take your time today, Margie my dear," she said. "I just wanted to pop in and wish you a Merry Christmas. I see that it is indeed! You have beautiful children Margie—they look like you! I come here at least once a week to visit your mother," she said without breaking the conversation. "Oh, she is such a lovely lady, and such a good listener! I enjoy telling her all my stories!"

Her eyes glimmered and were calming, mesmerizing. I looked towards my siblings and sensed they shared the same questions, but we were all unable to speak.

"I will be back tomorrow, Margie, for a longer visit. You have a wonderful Christmas!"

She bent down to kiss our mother's forehead and tears, not of sadness but of peace came to my eyes.

Chris was the first one to break the silence.

"Did we just see an angel? Like seriously, guys, did you see her? How did she get in here so quietly? Did you hear her, Diana?"

I shook my head. I had not found words just yet, which is unusual for me.

"I think she's an angel, do you guys?" asked Chris. "Even if she is a real person, she's like an angel that walks amongst us, you know?"

We nodded, all knowing that even if she wasn't an angel, she gave us a gift—to know that our mother wasn't alone when we could not be with her. Stranger or angel, I will never know, but the energy in the room shifted when she entered. A calm graced our hearts, allowing us space to enjoy our visit with our mother and each other.

Chapter 48

Caregivers

The stark realization that I was unable to care for Kim was a hard pill to swallow for me. It was obvious she needed more care than I could give her while working a full time job. The reality was crushing, but Kim somehow softened it.

"Diana, I want to move back to the farm," she stated on the drive back from the hospital. I was surprised, but I let her continue. "Now that we know what's going on with me, I don't feel crazy; I think I can handle Dad. We both know I need care."

"Dad can't be your caregiver, Kim," I said. "But I guess if I'm at work, neither can I."

The thought crushed me; I was defeated.

"Diana, you've cared for me my whole life, and I know you still will, just not every day anymore. I want to be with the animals and on the farm."

I was quiet as her words swept over me; I knew she is right. As the silence sat between the three of us, I thought of how I could line up a caregiver. Dad wouldn't be able to bathe her, help with bathroom issues or bedtime. The thoughts swam around in my mind until we pulled back into the farmyard. I knew I had to make some calls that week and figure out something so Kim could stay there.

It had been a long, emotionally exhausting day. As I walked back into our family home, I was greeted by the smell of a delicious meal yet again. Dad was sober and greeted us at the door. My mind tried to reckon why he didn't come support us, help us to deal with the emotions of the day. When I stopped to think about it, it seemed like when it really counted, he couldn't muster up the courage to do what needed to be done. I saw now that this was why I could: it was non-negotiable. It was not an option but a necessity.

We ate yet another delicious meal Trudy prepared and then enjoyed some playtime with Breanna. Dad asked us to line up by the fake fireplace for a picture. I didn't feel much like having a photo taken, but it had been years since we'd all been together or had a siblings picture taken. Trudy offered to take a picture of us all so Dad could be in it too. All I could think of was what next year would look like. *Would Kim be able to stand? To walk? To talk?* I brought myself back to the moment and did my best to let my thoughts not show on my face, which was a hard thing since I wore my emotions front and centre most days now. *Cheese!*

We needed to talk about our next step. Kim had shared her wishes with me, now I had to put them into action and get a plan framed up. Breanna and Kim had long since gone to bed, which left the discussions to the rest of us.

"Kim wants to move back to the farm; she told us on our way back from Kerrobert."

No one seemed surprised at the news because it was obvious I wouldn't be able to continue to take care of her, but the idea didn't quite sit well with me yet. In one way, I felt I had failed her and now I was drowning in a situation that offered little hope. Everyone understood and nodded in agreement.

"I am going to speak with a social worker, and we will need to line up money to hire a caregiver."

Trudy popped her head around the corner and chimed in, "I could take care of her for a while if you'd like."

I was surprised and speechless.

Dad jumped in. "It could work for a while until you get the funding figured out. In the meantime, you know?"

I gathered that they'd discussed this before, and everyone agreed that this would be our best (and really only) option for the time being. Her social worker and financial assistance was all through the Saskatoon office, so l needed a social worker from Kindersley. Even though I wouldn't be caring for Kim's daily needs, I would have to handle the financial and medical end of things. This offer eased my mind. I had a lot to work through and I knew it, but now I could grant Kim's wish and had somewhat of a plan.

"Who wants to come and see the neurologist with me in January? I got a letter a couple of days ago; the appointment is January 21."

Aaron gave me a nod; he would be there as I expected he would. I was not surprised. I promised to keep everyone in the loop on how things went with funding and the appointment. Then I pulled Trudy into the conversation to make sure she understood what she had just signed up for.

"There are moments when Kim suffers from severe psychosis, and we refer to these moments as Kim's 'ghosties.' They terrify her. She has a hard time distinguishing reality from what her mind is telling her and showing her. In those moments, I gently caress Kim's face, look directly into her eyes and speak softly to her. This is the only way to bring her back. She MUST take her medication, no questions asked, on time and proper dosage. If not, things can get out of hand really quickly."

"She seems good!" Trudy said, not understanding the illness (through no fault of her own). I had no idea what Dad had shared with her, but I also know that this would be a learn on the job situation. Dad and Aaron were also around to help guide when needed. I wasn't sure if Dad would be of much help, but I assured Trudy that I was only a phone call away.

"She is OK; far better than she was, but that is the heavy dose of medication she's on," I said. "The doctors may ease up on that if we find it is too heavy. As nice as it is to have her calm and easy to handle right now, I'm noticing some of her personality is suppressed, which isn't what we want either. We will know more on how best to handle the meds once we see the neurologist in Saskatoon in January."

I sensed Trudy might be feeling overwhelmed, especially since she didn't know the illness, but the idea of not being her caregiver overwhelmed me.

"Diana, I will be here. I've had her here for years," Dad said. "It's not like she just got sick when she was diagnosed; she's had this for a while."

Dad was right.

"Diana is looking into funding for a caregiver," Aaron said. "This takes time. Right now, there is no money for us to pay you, Trudy."

She assured us she was not doing it for the money, but I wasn't totally convinced. There was no time for doubt to creep in, though, as we didn't have any other options. Kim wanted to stay at the farm, and Dad could only do so much himself. The facts spoke for themselves. By the end of that evening, we determined that as long as Kim agreed to have Trudy tend to her while I lined up the rest, that this was how it would be for now. On one end, I felt relief knowing we had a plan. On the other end, I was conflicted. *Was this really the only option?* It also made me uncomfortable as it forced me to trust my dad, which was very difficult.

Brent and I stayed a couple of days longer and managed to get some visits in with some friends and family in the area. It was nice to be enveloped in their comfort and understanding. When life knocked me down, I noticed there were many people to help pick me and my family up. That was one thing I started to notice that was different from when I grew up in Plenty; people seemed to genuinely understand the battle our family faced because they knew Mom and had seen first hand what we had been through. There was no need to explain, it just was. The quiet comfort in not having to explain what this disease meant and how deeply it would take hold was a small gift to me. I had a hard enough time talking about Kim's illness, but explaining what would happen to her to people who hadn't seen it first hand just made it that much more difficult.

Chapter 49

What's Next?

Kim didn't want to leave Gizmo again, so she decided not to come back to St. Brieux with us. We would pack up her stuff and bring it down in the following weeks. Aaron planned to bring Kim to Saskatoon for her appointment with the neurologist, and I would meet them there.

The snow crunched under our tires as we left the snow-covered yard, without Kim, and I leaned my head against the passenger side window. Having said goodbye to Kimberley moments before, I felt out of my body. It was strange, uncomfortable. Guilt washed over me at the thought that she was shackled back at the place that once broke her, broke all of us. I felt sick to my stomach.

The four-hour drive provided lots of opportunity for me to dance back in time to what I never knew would be considered "simpler" times. One memory seeped to the surface and swept me into a daydream as the car glided over the bumpy Saskatchewan pavement.

Once upon a time I took a picture that I now think of as foreshadowing. Supper was cleaned up as Kim and I prepared for a good game of Crazy Eights at the dining room table. As I looked out the window, I couldn't believe what the sky had painted across it!

"Kimberley, do you see what I see?" I shouted.

I got up and moved to the south-facing window. Being a creative like me, Kim replied, "Oh my, it is Jesus in the clouds, Diana!" She saw what I saw right away! We could only explain it as God in the clouds. I quickly found Dad's 35mm camera that he rarely let us use and even more rarely developed the film from so I could capture this moment! The clouds formed into the shape of God while the farm buildings had become silhouetted from the sunset.

"Whoa, this is crazy!" Kim gasped as we stood in awe in what felt like God's presence.

Kim was more of a devout Christian than I, her faith never wavered. Standing under the pinks, purples and blues of the south sky, I slid the expensive camera out of its case as gingerly as I could, removed the lens cap and began trying to document on film what was dancing above me in the sky. We rushed to the front lawn in hopes of a better angle to depict this cloud, and I could only hope the pictures would capture the face we saw in the clouds. *The face is unmistakable. Two eyes, nose, beard flowing down and hair flowing up. This is incredible!*

I was not deeply religious, but I did believe. I had enjoyed youth group and attending church with some friends. What I saw there appeared to be either God himself or Jesus. Kim and I talked over one another as we pointed to the features we each saw.

"Look, there's his eyes!" I squealed in delight.

"That has got to be his hair," Kimberley said, pointing out what she was seeing.

It was unmistakable. Indeed, there was a face in the clouds looking down on our farm. I took several photos as Kim continued to share what she thought it meant.

"Diana, it's like God is protecting us! He knows we haven't had it easy, and He wants us to know He is watching over us!"

Kimberley was the better person to understand the omen the clouds were depicting, but all I could think of was *One day this picture is going to be my book cover.* We sat in silence for a little longer, watching the cloud change formation and melt back into the horizon as we allowed the messages of the cloud to penetrate our souls.

I was jolted out of my daydream as Brent and I approached Saskatoon. He pulled me back to the present, but my mind lingered with the thoughts of that photo. *Where did that picture end up? I need it for my book cover. When will I ever have time to finish my book? I started it in high school and haven't touched it since Kim got sick. Maybe I never will.*

Chapter 50

History Repeated

Brent and I had started to talk about moving back to Cudworth where his family lived. This meant we would commute about two hours round trip to and from work each day but it was important to us to be closer to family, especially his aging parents. We hadn't told anyone, but we had looked at this little yellow house we drove by on our way to Brent's parents' house. It was just through the back alley and would be nice and close. It would also put us an hour closer to Kim, which was important to me. Even though we had things to do in our personal lives, it seemed like Kim's needs were always on the front burner; it left little time for Brent and me.

My focus should have been wedding planning. We got engaged, and in the midst of chaos and emotional upheaval, we were planning a wedding for September (I know, bad farmer's daughter that I am). Kim would be one of my maids of honour along with my best friend, Lindsay. I was convinced Kim would be limited in her abilities by the time the wedding came, even though it was only nine months away. We had booked the hall and caterer and bought my dress. Bridesmaid's dress material had been picked up and dropped off at the seamstress.

Things were humming along, but our wedding plans were not at the forefront of my mind. The heaviest weight on my mind was Kim's neurologist appointment the next day, and all I wanted to do was get through that day. Illness in any form is heavy, as was the grief I was starting to process. Reality was mashing up with my past in a very scary and real way, and as much as I wanted to engage the "flight" activity of my brain just as my dad had, something else sat inside my heart and mind: knowing that I would fight this as hard as I could.

I would bring some of Kim's belongings tomorrow because I knew she missed her bedding and teddy bears. She was still docile, not really herself; Dad had noticed and commented on it too. One of my top priorities when we saw the neurologist was to sort her medication out. I missed the Kim who used to joke around and have some fun. Now she seemed like a zombie that was going through the motions of the day, expressionless. Seeing the neurologist made me all nervous even though I knew the MRI results. No surprises there. I was more concerned about how to move forward on treating an illness when we didn't even have the basics covered, like a name. I knew what would happen to Kim, but I didn't know how to fight a battle against a nameless disease. It felt like trying to win a fight in the pitch black of the night against an opponent I couldn't see. This disease was full of paradoxes.

I confirmed with Aaron and Kim that we would meet downtown at 10:30 and the appointment was at 11:00. I got off work at 4:00 the day before and packed up Kim's bedroom. She wanted the purple bedding as well as some of the trinkets from her nightstand and dresser. The furniture would have to wait for Aaron to come as we didn't have a truck. I put her clothes in her larger luggage duffle bag, the same one I'd packed three times before, and we hauled everything into my black Chevy Celebrity so I was ready to leave first thing in the morning. Everyone needed to be on the road early. I mentioned to Aaron that mornings were not Kim's best time because she had always been a deep sleeper and it is hard to rouse her. That may actually be OK so the neurologist would see her in a state that was more accurate. He assured me he would get her there and Trudy would be around to help her get ready.

I woke up anxious the next morning as I pushed the blankets back and swung my legs over the side of the bed. This was just the beginning of a long line of appointments to come. As I walked to the bathroom to get ready, the feelings of where we were just a little over a month before caught up with me. The water ran warm out of the faucet as my tears cascaded down and washed down the drain. Sometimes in this world there were things we did not want to face; we wish that others stood up at the plate and took the bat so we didn't have to do it. Today was one of those days. I wanted someone to run the bases because it was difficult to run when I knew the outcome. This was a game that couldn't be won.

Thoughts bounced around my mind as I pulled onto the 368 and headed north to Highway 41. A recent conversation with a social worker about funding for Kim's caregiver came to mind. She said the government of Saskatchewan wanted to keep people with caregivers in their homes longer due to the costs of "in-care." I had set up an appointment in Kindersley in early February to work through this paperwork, if possible.

My mind ran on overdrive when I thought of all the things I needed to handle for Kim's care. Even though she was no longer living with me directly, there was much to be done. We had to add power of attorney to the list, and Kim had asked me to be her medical and financial directive. At twenty-four, I was nervous about the idea, but it was really no different than what I'd been doing already. Once this paperwork was finalized, Dad would no longer be left with the task of signing her Do Not Resuscitate form. That would be my job. I took these hard parts of caregiving from my father for two reasons. Partly to do with feeling guilty that I was not sick myself and also because of the deep compassion I carried in my heart for my dad. He had already been through far too much, so I shouldered what I could. I spoke to the lawyers my dad used in Kindersley, and the papers had been drafted.

I found a place to park on 4th Avenue downtown. I was not a fan of parallel parking, so I located a parkade three blocks away where I could pay three dollars and park all day. I didn't know how long this would take, probably not three hours, but this was how desperately I hated parallel parking! Of course, on my walk over to the Sturdy Stone, I saw several street parking spots and laughed quietly to myself.

"Where did you park, the mall?" Aaron teased as I approached, and we laughed.

"I may as well have! Maybe you can give me a ride back to my car after we're done," I said as we stood in front of his truck, which was directly in front of the Sturdy Stone!

Of course, the parking Gods were on his side today! Maybe I just needed some confidence. I noted that this was usually a conversation Kim would giggle at, but her face was blank; it had been since the medication dosage was increased in December. Kim was here in body, but she had become a ghost, which was something we would address.

We sat down in three black chairs with arm rests. There were magazines from 1988 with articles and pictures of all the best rock bands. Bon Jovi was on the cover. Aaron and I went to Bon Jovi when I was in high school, and I'd been a big fan for many years. We shared a giggle because it was 2003 and these magazines were in pretty good shape! I found the article and made light conversation about music until we were called in.

"Kirk, Kimberley," the dry clinical voice called to the room full of patients and their loved ones.

We knew there would be a physical examination first, and Aaron had asked to stay out of that in the event there were any uncomfortable moments. I exchanged pleasantries with a tall, middle-aged nurse and followed her into a small, white and grey examining room. I helped Kimberley onto the paper covered examining table, and I noticed her foot did not immediately lift to the stool used to help patients get onto the bed. I bent down and moved her foot in place so she could safely board the table. Posters that looked nearly as old as the magazine in the waiting room decorated the walls.

"Kimberley will next be examined physically by Dr. Anderson," the nurse informed us.

As he entered the room, I noticed he was an elderly gentleman with smooth silver hair, a white lab coat and a stethoscope around his neck, worn like a scarf. I sensed his wisdom and immediately felt at ease in his presence, something few doctors had achieved with me.

He was pleasant and gentle with Kim as he worked her body and mind though the standard neurology examination, exactly the same as what Dr. Wind performed almost a year before. This time I saw significant deterioration of her co-ordination. Her walk was unsteady, and the hand-to-nose test was a complete miss. I was no longer able to watch her fail this exam worse than the first time, and my eyes fell to the floor along with my tears. I quickly pulled my hand to my cheeks and brushed the tears aside, hoping no one had noticed. I was not a public crier, especially in front of a stranger, but this illness had pulled my emotions to the surface. I was hit with a wave of tears and grief at the most random times, crashing about my heart with the impact of a tsunami. There was no simple way to say how cruel this mystery illness was. Soon she would be a shell, a soul locked in a broken mind and body. The thought sent chills coursing through my body, and I shuddered. I was brought back from my thoughts by the doctor.

"How have you been feeling lately?" he asked.

"Really good," Kim responded.

Looking up, I made eye contact with the doctor and shook my head.

He looked back at Kimberley and said, "Have you noticed anything out of the ordinary lately? Perhaps some trouble walking?"

"No," she said.

The questioning proved pointless, but Dr. Anderson smiled nonetheless, dismissing us to his office but requesting Kim take a break and sit out the next part. We left the room and walked back towards the full waiting room. I motioned towards Aaron saying,

"My brother is here too." Aaron quickly followed behind me after I delivered Kim back to the nurse at the front.

"See that she is comfortable and taken care of please, Sherry," the doctor said, still smiling. "It was very nice to meet with you Ms. Kirk. The nurse here will take care of you for a little while so I can discuss things with your siblings. Is that OK, Kimberley?"

The doctor didn't wait for her response, he simply nodded and nudged her forward towards the nurse. The nurse got up from her desk while slipping paperwork back into a slender manila folder.

"Of course. Right this way, Ms. Kimberley. My oh my, don't you have the most perfectly slender fingers and nails," the nurse commented.

Just like our mother's, I thought. Kim's fingernails had been a long-standing jealousy on my end. Perfectly shaped and painted, Kim announced that her caregiver gave her a manicure before coming.

We left Kim behind and wound our way down the narrow halls and into a generously lit office. Two chairs were placed in front of the desk which faced a large, frosted window. The winter sunshine glistened brightly through. The sunshine in Saskatchewan is one of the few beauties I find comfort in during the long, cold winter months. The sunshine danced into a kaleidoscope of colours as it hit the prism dangling elegantly from the top of the window frame. The colours mesmerized me, and for a moment I forgot where I was and what I was doing. It was peaceful.

Aaron and Dr. Anderson exchanged a handshake before both pulled their chairs out to be seated.

"Aaron, Diana, I have read extensively through your mom's file and studied Kim's MRI. As you know, the news isn't good."

It felt like I had to will myself to continue to breathe as I forced myself to focus and listened closer.

"There is extensive atrophy already in the brain. This is something I have not seen in my career."

He has to be in his late sixties, I thought. *This is not reassuring and not what I wanted to hear.*

"Her cerebellum seems quite deteriorated, along with some of the frontal lobe, compromising both memory and movement."

This made total sense.

"As you saw from her examination today, Diana, her skill set is failing. How would you compare what you saw today to her first neuro exam last year?"

I fumbled around in my brain for the right word and managed to reply, "Today was far worse. Her skills are deteriorating. She was an artist before, but now she can barely write her name legibly. Her eye contact is sporadic, her movements are much like our mother's were, rigid."

"Tell me more about your mother, I am curious to know," he prodded. "I see from her records, much like Kim, they don't verbalize the troubles they were having, such as with walking or writing, at least to the medical team. From reading your mother's record, she and Kimberley seem to parallel one another. Am I correct with this?"

Aaron detailed what he recalled about Mom's behaviours from when we were younger, tying many things to Kimberley's current state. His memory bank was far deeper than mine as I had no memory of a healthy mother and nothing to compare her against. Everything Aaron said was exactly what we were going through with Kim.

"Unfortunately, kids, due to the fact that this is an extremely rare disease, we will not be taking Kimberley on as a patient," Dr. Anderson said, his voice softened with compassion.

My jaw dropped. *What the hell do you expect us to do?* I think to myself.

"Don't worry, though, I have a plan. It's not as convenient as coming to Saskatoon, but I have lined up the top neurology team in western Canada to deal with this case at the Movement Disorders Program located at the Foothills Hospital in Calgary. They are the best neuro team, and they have agreed to take your sister on. I know it is a lot of driving, which could be a challenge for Kimberley, but I also know they run clinics in Medicine Hat about once a month to see a portion of our Saskatchewan residents who cannot make the trip to Calgary. So there are options. Is taking Kim to Calgary an option for you? She will need to be seen every few months."

Most of these trips would fall on my shoulders as her primary decision maker, and I knew it. I was sure that Aaron would step in as well when necessary. I wanted this responsibility. I was the only woman not to get sick in the Kirk family, and I felt an obligation to provide a voice and be an advocate.

"Yes, of course. Whatever I have to do, I will," I said, nodding.

"Great! I am sure you will not regret this decision. We have her booked in for March 1, it's the earliest appointment, in Calgary. Do you think you can make it?" he asked.

"Of course. I will make every appointment," I promised.

"Excellent! Kimberley is lucky to have you. Now, do you folks have any questions for me?" he inquired.

"If you reference Dr. Abba's records on our mother, he stated that this appeared to be a rare genetic disease with no previous history," I said. "Therefore, Dr. Abba concluded that none of Margie's kids would get this illness. That is a bold statement and clearly wrong. If there was no known cause and no name, why would a neurologist make such a statement? My dad went the past twenty-four years thinking his kids were going to be OK; he even told us we had nothing to worry about! And now we are here. How does that happen?"

"Well, Diana, I cannot speak on behalf of a fellow neurologist, but you are right, that statement is reaching, to say the least. Especially since there is still no name and not enough was known about it. This was an error of judgement to put that in writing, Diana, and rest assured these are the things that the team of neurologists will not do when you see them in Calgary. We are all professionals, but when dealing with an unknown illness, it is best practice to err on the side of caution. Speculation, such as what you see in this letter, should have never been expressed. I am sure your father had this question for the neurologist, and perhaps he was empathic to your father's situation and was likely trying to give him hope in a time when there was little positive to hold on to. It can be difficult when a doctor is faced with a case as challenging as your mother's; she was young, with all of you at home to care for. Your father would have had to step into a role that wasn't the cultural norm at the time. Keep in mind that we as medical professionals are only ever doing what we feel is best for the patient and their families. As much as this letter probably upsets you, remember that this does nothing to change what your family is now facing."

I nodded in agreement; everything he said made sense. I was holding onto that one small bit of information in anger, knowing it really made no difference. That letter was written in late December 1978, twenty-four years before.

"I know what to expect with this illness, but I want to know if there is a chance it may not be as bad for Kim as it was for mom," I said. "Is there a chance this may not be as serious; a milder form? How bad is the MRI?"

As if expecting this question, Dr. Anderson provided me with a prepared reply. "Sadly, no. The atrophy, which is to say, shrinking, of the brain is significant already. As you saw, Kimberley's abilities are already quite limited. I've compared her scans to your mother's, the latest one is quite old, from 1986. From what I see, Kimberley's atrophy closely mimics that of your mother's. Whether she will continue to atrophy at the same pace as your mother is hard to say for sure. If we go off of your mother's scans and charts and the recount that you, Diana, gave the neurology team during Kim's stay at the Handleman ward, I wouldn't hesitate to stand with the idea that what happened to your mother is happening to your sister, and the modelling looks to be on pace for similar atrophy. The brain will continue to atrophy in the future, but you will receive more in-depth information when you visit Calgary."

I sensed we were near the end of the appointment, and I needed to bring up one more crucial item: Kim's medication.

"I have noticed Kim isn't really Kim anymore since the doctors put her on a heavy dose of anti-psychotic medication. She is more like a zombie, no personality. Normally she is joking and quite funny. Yes, she is generally quiet, but this is different. She has no reaction. Do we have any other options to explore?"

I felt I was respectful yet definite in how I pushed for answers. He was quiet for a few moments while he pondered the paperwork in front of him. They had taken all her vitals, weight and whatnot when we arrived, so he calculated out the dosage that was prescribed.

"I think we have something that would probably work far better for Kimberley," he said. "It is also an anti-psychosis drug, but it shouldn't suppress her mood as much."

He scribbled something I couldn't read on his prescription pad, then explained, in great detail, how to safely move Kim from one medication to the other. It had to be done with care, so we decided I would be around when we made the switch. With that, we concluded our meeting.

As we walked to the waiting room, Aaron and I exchanged glances; more waiting, and this time the answers were outside of the province. I knew they were the experts, but I still did not like to hear that there were no doctors in Saskatchewan that would touch this illness. It was simply too complex. On the plus side, though, the medication change should help bring back the Kim we knew and loved. She was a body walking around, so agreeable (believe me, I'm not complaining about that part), but it was just not who she was, and I missed the girl who teased and got her back up sometimes.

It was after noon and we were all hungry, so Aaron decided we may as well hit up somewhere for lunch. I reminded him we should pick up Kim's prescription first, and Kim was tired but agreeable. We sat down at Mullberry's, and I noticed Kim hadn't asked about what we learned at the appointment. I decided to fill her in.

"We will be heading to Calgary for your first appointment with an amazing neuro team that will help us on March1" I said.

She seemed distant, with no real reaction to this news. I reminded myself about the prescriptions in my purse, which left me hopeful that we would find a better balance.

"We can stay in a hotel with a pool!"

Kim's eyes brightened. "Is Brent going to come too?" she asked, now grinning.

"Of course! I will book it this week!"

With that, we finished our lunch, Aaron dropped me off at my car and we parted ways.

As I travelled back home, I contemplated how we would pay for this trip to Calgary; I had already taken days off, and unless I took a holiday, I wouldn't get paid. I racked my brain and was reminded of a travel allowance one of the social workers informed me of last year. It was an allowance for medical trips. I made a mental note to check on this because I knew I could not ask Dad for money he wouldn't have.

Chapter 51

Movement Disorder Clinic

Brent and I did the first leg of the trip to Calgary, from St. Brieux to Plenty, the night before picking up Kim, so we were at Dad's farmhouse by 6:00 a.m. that day. Kim was happy to see us, but Dad was visibly stressed, not an uncommon look for him, but the energy in the house had shifted.

"Diana, Trudy wants to be paid for taking care of Kim," Dad said as I walked into the kitchen.

He was standing by the stove, making some oatmeal for breakfast.

"What?" I said, a little too loudly. *Ah. This is what I was sensing—tension between Dad and Trudy.* "Dad, I don't have all the paperwork done yet. I just got the power of attorney papers, the government has everything, but we are at their mercy."

My panicked voice showed the mental strain I tried to keep at bay when around Dad. I had made some big noise about doing a better job with Kim than he did with mom, so I preferred to hide my weakness or fears. Dad knew I was right and nodded in agreement.

"I know, it's just that she keeps asking for money!"

I appreciated she was helping us with Kim and recalled all the conversations where she would not hear of taking money, but apparently things had changed.

"Nothing is ever simple with this!" I said, already on edge because of the appointment in Calgary and the big drive ahead. I shook my head. "Dad, what do you expect me to do? We have no extra funds! Brent and I are spending our money for the gas and hotel for this trip, and I have to put a claim in to get it back. I have had to take so much time off work to deal with all of this and that affects my pay cheque."

Dad knew this, too, and I instantly felt bad for burdening him. *This is not HIS problem to deal with*, I thought. When hard things occurred in the family, I felt obligated to take them on because of my tremendous guilt for causing my mother's illness and remaining healthy myself. I was trying to earn my keep with my family. Mom and Kim were saddled with the nameless disease, so I would take on everything else.

"I provide her with free room and board, free food and gas. Seems like enough to me," Dad said.

I looked down at my silver watch and saw that the little hand was at nine; time to wake Kim.

"Dad, we will have to continue this later. I've got to get Kim up and we need to head out." I swept the crumbs from my toast into my hand, dusted them on the plate and walked into the kitchen. "I'll be back to wash these up," I said, depositing the dishes in the sink.

"Don't worry about the dishes," Dad said.

Kim's bedroom door was closed when I reached the top of the staircase, and I turned the familiar gold knob and entered the brightly-lit purple bedroom. When the snow glistened in the sunshine, the whole room was enveloped in it—I loved it! Kim had stuffed herself rather disjointedly amongst the sheets and blankets. You would never know there was a person under there.

I sat down quietly at the edge of her bed, my hand naturally reaching for what I assumed was her shoulder. I gently caressed it and quietly spoke her to wakefulness, careful not to upset or jolt her into fear. Her hair was a big mess as she pulled herself from her cocoon. Laughing now, I saw her face break from confusion to happiness as her steel blue eyes met mine.

"Time to get up, Kimberley! We've got a big drive ahead of us!"

She looked rather confused, so I said, "Today is the day we leave for Calgary and get to stay in the hotel! We never do that!"

As she got ready, I noted the unsteadiness in her movements, which tended to be more pronounced when she was tired. It had been like that since the diagnosis, and she no longer fought what the illness was doing to her body. She accepted it, but I hadn't. I wouldn't allow her to give up on herself.

The winding road south and west was long and beautiful. We made it to Cactus Corner before everyone needed a stretch and a pee. We filled up with gas then decided to go through Drumheller, the scenic route. It was a beautiful drive, even in March. I was grateful for the good weather as we pulled up to the Travelodge in Calgary. It was a lot for Brent and I to navigate our way through Calgary with our map, but we made it. I liked to travel, and I always familiarized myself with street and highway names and numbers—a little reassurance that we would make it to our destination. We checked in and found our room near the end of the long, dimly-lit hallway on the third floor.

Weaving the luggage and ourselves though the doorway, we were greeted with a pleasant and tidy room. The rugs showed their age, but the fresh paint made the place look clean, a must-have trait. A table with a lamp separated two queen beds. Staying in a hotel as a child was a luxury I never experienced, so even staying in one as an adult was a novelty. Kimberley had childlike wonder and fascination in her eyes! She had been so much more herself since we found the right medication. Her spirit had been dulled, but it was now back. *She is happy*, I thought to myself, and that happiness enwrapped my heart and then sent soul-soothing coos to the achy guilt that hadn't subsided since the diagnosis—*Why her? Why not me?* Hunger pulled me from my thoughts.

"Time to order some pizza!" I said, my elbow gently rubbing Kim's rib in child's play.

This trip had us in the tight grasp of this unknown illness and searching for answers, but I was determined to do what I did best—*make the best out of it*—so it was important to lighten the mood whenever we got the chance.

After the pizza arrived, I realized we didn't have plates or napkins, so I called the front desk. Brent was washing up in the bathroom, and I decided I couldn't wait for the front desk to bring the plates and napkins; I dove right in, satisfying the hunger beast within. Brent entered the room and looked around.

"Where's Kim?" he said.

Tilting my head in confusion, I wiped the oozing pizza sauce off my bottom lip and looked around. I had no answer. In fact, I hadn't noticed she was gone! Frantic, I flung open the hotel room door with an aggressive pull. My eyes scanned the dimly-lit halls, but I did not see her. Brent was fast behind me with my shoes and a hotel room key. He would stay put in case she found her way back while I went searching. I had no idea where to begin.

"Call the front desk and tell them!" I yelled at Brent as the elevator door shut. "She can't leave this hotel!"

My imagination is a strength and a weakness, and it was working overtime. *What if someone picked her up? What if she is on the street! This is Calgary, a huge city, I have no idea where to look and she has no idea where to go!* Tears begged to fall as I raced towards the stairs after scanning the hall. I hastily pulled my long sleeve to my eyes, brushing away outward evidence of my fears. I stopped at the second floor hoping Brent had alerted the front desk. *What was she wearing?: Purple sweater, jeans, pink boots. She loves those fluffy imitation Ugg boots of hers! Did she actually put them on? Did she grab a coat?* Questions bogged down my mind as I scanned the second floor—nothing. That means she has made it to the main level, so perhaps the staff have her there.

I flew back to the staircase and down to the first floor, thoughts chasing me. *The main floor has way more areas to scan than a couple of hallways. The pool or gym—worst case—the street!* Just then, my airways began to defy me as they had for so many years. Stress and asthma are arch enemies. Add in some physical exertion and I was in trouble. My slender olive-toned hand slid into my pocket, fingers frantically searching. My Ventolin inhaler must have been in the hotel room. Unable to breathe, I forced myself to keep going. I had to find Kim!

I entered the main floor to the right of the elevators and saw nothing. I sprinted to the front desk where I was greeted by two individuals who are not nearly as panicked as me.

"These guys have no clue what we are dealing with," I accidently said out loud.

"Mam, are you searching for your sister? What is she is wearing?"

Their speech felt too slow—we had no time.

"Dark hair, purple shirt, jeans, pink boots. I don't know if she's wearing a jacket. If she is, it's white. I take it you haven't seen her?"

"No, Miss. I was on the phone."

I asked them to scan the rest of the main floor while I ran towards the sliding doors and the parking lot. That's when I saw her. No shoes, no jacket, in the snow. The relief I felt is hard to put to words. I stopped dead in my tracks, succumbing to my asthma while calling her name. Kim did not move. She was what we lovingly referred to as "spaced out." As the worker from the front desk approached me, I breathlessly told her to call up to Room 322, tell Brent we found her and to bring my inhaler.

Back in our room, Kim was disoriented and confused as to where we were. She knew who I was, but that did little to console me after this fiasco. My lungs had opened up and allowed air back inside after taking my medication. She sat on the bed as I changed her socks, her feet cubes of ice from standing outside in the cold snow. Shock had locked away our words and our hunger, as the pizza sits, cold, exactly where we left it. The plates remained in the hall. Kim was very cold, so I drew her a warm bath. This would give Brent and I a chance to talk about how to handle her going forward.

"She gets the far bed. We lock the door, both locks. I won't sleep," I said.

It was the only solution I could come up with. We couldn't take the chance that she gets out again.

"If she does, she could die," I report starkly to Brent, who already knew this possible outcome.

He also understood we had little choice. The front desk was aware, but we could not rely on them to pay attention.

Kim finished her bath and announced she was hungry. I picked up the plates from the hallway and brought them inside. I noticed she was back to herself, smiling and laughing at *The Flintstones* on the TV. Glad to have her safe and sound, we all decided to eat.

This proved to be one of the longest nights of my life. I usually liked my sleep and a good hotel stay, but I was on night watch. I tried to keep still so as not to wake Brent, but I sensed he was equally tense. Without my glasses or contacts, all I could see were the fuzzy red lines of the clock, and guessing the time kept me awake. My mind began conjuring all sorts of haunting thoughts, so it's like I'm in a waking nightmare. I can escape during sleep, but there was no reprieve that night.

Sleep called my name around 5:30 in the morning, and our appointment was at 10:30. The hotel was about a twenty-minute drive taking traffic into account, so we planned to leave at 9:30 to give ourselves a little extra time.

Brent brought up some juice and snacks from the complimentary breakfast. Kim was slow out of the gate and had bags under her eyes. My gut told me this was okay because the doctors would get more of a true indication of what Kim battles. She was far worse when she was tired. I planned to ask for a sleep aid to be added to her medication regiment because it was important she got rest.

I laid the map out on the bed as I stuffed part of a blueberry muffin in my mouth and chased it with orange juice. I needed to focus and plan our route. I would drive, Brent would navigate, Kim would sit in the back.

We left the hotel room a mess of pizza, muffins and other items strewn about on unmade beds. Booking for two nights was a good idea, especially since none of us slept well. After the appointment, we could come back to the hotel for a rest, do a little shopping, have a nice meal and relax in the hot tub. I was sure we would need it.

I was lost in thought as we drove past buildings and nature in equal measure. Calgary had always been a beautiful city. Nestled on the edge of the foothills, you could see the Rocky Mountains on a clear day, a dollop of snow delicately placed on top like a sundae! Brent studied the map as I drove. Kim was chirping away in the back seat, giving us a play-by-play of the majestic scenery.

"Look, guys, the Calgary Tower! Diana, do you remember when Jean and Scottie took us there as kids? You wanted to drop a penny from there and Scotty said it could hurt someone from so far up! That was a great trip!"

That trip to Calgary when we were young was one of my favourite holidays (not that there were many holidays as kids). I was grateful she brought it to mind as I had felt anxious all morning. *Ah, the good ole' days.* Kim pulled my mind into the past as we reminisced over the first time we saw these wonderous creations of nature back when we were eight and ten. We stayed with our dad's cousin, Jean, and her family for three weeks in Calgary and ventured out to Banff one day. Kim giggled as she recalled the drive back from Banff when they stopped to pick up a stranded lady and her child on the side of the road.

"We really ought to call them next time we're in town, Kim," I said. "They have always been so good to us."

Her heart sung with a gleeful, "Yes! And maybe we can go back out to those mountains! They are so cool!"

She was right. There was just something about the mountains that pulled me in; they slowed my heart and calmed my mind. I wished we had booked another day to explore them in the winter, but we had to get back to work. My boss had been so good about me taking time off, but we needed the money. We couldn't afford trips. Still, I enjoyed Kim's joyful dance with daydreams of sunshine, waterfalls and crisp mountain air.

Back in reality, I was pleased that by some small miracle we pulled into the parking lot at the Foothills Hospital without making any wrong turns! I thanked the Lord for small victories!

"I'm going to wait in here for you guys," Brent said while he opened the passenger door and slid his seat forward so Kim could get out.

I pulled my seat forward and grabbed both our purses. Kim's purse was pale pink with the word "QUEEN" bedazzled across it. It was an interesting fashion choice for someone so quiet, but at least it matched her boots. Since my stint working in a high-fashion clothing store for women, I felt I had an eye for fashion whereas Kim had more of an eye for art. Funny, for a girl that never liked pink, I was rather surprised in her shopping choices recently. Content, Kim rounded the green Grand Am to meet me. Even though she looked exhausted, she had a smile on her face. This trait, bravery in the face of adversity, was something we Kirk kids learned well.

"Buck up," I heard my dad chime in my mind.

That's code for "No tears." Kim had numbed her emotions her whole life whereas I wore it all—sadness, anger, joy, sorrow, grief, happiness, curiosity and so much more—on my sleeve. This was a bone of contention with my dad because emotions made him uncomfortable. Conformity was an expectation, not an option. I was built just the opposite. I was able to share my feelings once I moved away from the farm, although I hid my tears because of shame. I started authentically letting my heart sing or cry, depending on the emotions stirring my soul and move me to my next right move. I was unsure how to share my emotions when I was a kid. The only time Dad revealed any of his sadness was when he made it to the bottom of a bottle. Other than that, he usually had one mood: anger.

I knew there were times I had to protect my heart so I could get through the motions of a moment or a day—today was a day that required armour. So I did the unnatural, assumed a stonewalled composure and walked into the building. The long glass hallways were brightly-lit, and soul-soothing sunshine cascaded over us just like it used to when Kim and I laid on the grass as kids and found shapes in the clouds for hours. It felt like a good place. I took it as a good omen that it was sunny; it somehow made the day more palatable, less doom and gloom.

A sharp right at the end of the hall led into the Movement Disorders Clinic where we checked in. The staff was attentive and compassionate as they led us down a maze of halls and into the examination room. All examination rooms tended to look the same—sterile with some random information affixed to the walls. The posters in this room were about neurological disorders like Parkinson's disease and Multiple Sclerosis. The wait was notably shorter because they were not meeting with people battling a cold or broken bone, so no one got put ahead of us there. Broken brains, that was their niche, and I was keenly aware of the power of a place like this. *They can help us.*

The door-knob turned slowly and a team of white coats entered the room.

"Do all neurologists work in groups?" I gently joked to break the ice.

They broke into smiles.

"Ms. Kirk?" the head neurologist asked, seeing two of us.

"I'm Diana Kirk, and this is my sister, your patient, Kimberley Kirk."

We exchanged handshakes as I stood.

"This is Dr. Raft, I am Dr. Okasaqua, head of neurology. We are your team of doctors, Kimberley. Today we will go through a few things together, then discuss some things. Is this okay with you, Kimberley?" he said respectfully and professionally.

Kim nodded.

"Sounds good," I said.

"Now I see here you're from Saskatchewan. Where is Plenty?"

Kim, on a good day, looked to me.

"It's northeast of Kindersley," I said.

Dr. Okasaqua moved towards the chair where Kim was sitting and said, "Let's move you up onto this examination table."

Kim got up shakily, and the doctors helped her move across to the table. Either she was very nervous or her tremors were more noticeable.

"Good," Dr. Okasaqua said. "Very good."

She patted Kim's hand in reassurance but we all knew that this simple task was, in fact, not good. But there is something to be said for a good bedside manner, and this doctor certainly had it.

The physical exam was the same as all the rest and confirmed what we already knew, but she had gotten worse. The nose test was usually a failure, but this time she missed the mark completely, her finger failing to touch her own nose, let alone the doctor's. Shock spread across my face as the doctor, as if sensing this, turned and caught my expression. I made a mental note to round back to this, as she nodded in a silent agreement.

More testing, more failures. Kim was exhausted from the restless sleep, the miles we travelled and all the questions. Like previous times, though, she had little to complain of regarding her abilities, or lack thereof, just like she was with the neurologist in Saskatoon. Her brain scans and I were the only ones who told her story.

Next, they ask about our parents. I remained silent, my ears perked. Kim's "facts" were, as expected, disjointed and jumbled, and did not paint a picture of our parents. It did not take long before they realized the line of questioning was futile, so the nurse came back into the room and said, "Come along, Kimberley, let's get your measurements." Judging the air in the room, I stayed put; it was time for me to share what I knew.

"How do you feel that went, Diana?" Dr. Okasaqua inquired.

"Not good," I simply stated, emotions working their way to the surface.

I fumbled clumsily through my purse to find a tissue. I knew this day would be hard, but nothing prepared me for just how hard.

"Correct. Now Diana, I need to reassure you that as rare as this illness is, this is what we deal with here. Your sister is lucky to have you to speak for her. I see the bond between you two is strong. Not everyone is lucky enough to have an advocate."

She paused, waiting for me to respond, but I could not; too much to digest at the moment. My silent nod motioned her to continue.

"That being said, can you please fill in the gaps with your mother? Does Kim model her completely?"

"Not completely," I started, choking back the tears from this devastating diagnosis. "Kim has far more psychosis than Mom. She sees her 'ghosties,' and they terrorize her. Mom wasn't like that. Well, if she was, it's not something I saw or people talked about. Dad said it started with her shuffling her feet, not able to pick them up. He said he'd tell her to pick up her feet, but she'd continue to shuffle along. It slowed them down. Forgetfulness was another big thing; she burned things on the stove as she didn't remember she was cooking. That was the scariest to Dad; he thought she may burn the whole house down with us kids in it when he was in the field. As you probably read, she was diagnosed December 10, 1978, and Kim was diagnosed twenty-six years later to the day."

The doctor put her hands to her mouth as if pulling her jaw back up off the floor. That fact still floored me every time I heard those words pass my lips. As it sank in, I was pulled into thoughts of a future full of the same patterns our mother took.

"When did your mom stop talking, Diana?"

I inhaled deeply at the question. This was the part of the disease that bothered me the most. *I have no memory of my mom completing an entire sentence in my life. She never once told me she loved me.*

"By the time I started forming memories, her word use was limited. She would say 'Yes' or 'No' mostly. My dad would ask her to say everyone's names while he pointed us out, but she never remembered mine, always calling me 'Aaron.'"

It infuriated me. As an adult I knew this wasn't intentional, but my formative years with the most influential woman in my life were marred with the stain of being forgotten. Sharing this with the doctor was like watching the perfect storm emerge from within, pulling me apart. Tears broke past the barricade of my eyelids, spilling over like the tumultuous waves of pain inside me. White coats are professional, but I knew the level of pain they witnessed in their patients and their families. I was struggling to keep my composure. Dr. Okasaqua's eyes met mine and she reached her hand out and enveloped mine as I shook. She was human, and I really saw that for the first time.

Doctors always held a high regard in my young mind because they were able to fix things most of us could not. They were smart and sophisticated as far as I was concerned. In that moment while looking in her sapphire blue eyes, I sensed her soul and knew she was just like me and doing her best to help.

The line of questioning continued for a while longer, but she moved from the heaviness of childhood to the situation we were facing; not that it was any easier or better. However, I felt some hope that maybe science had progressed and could do something to help. I kept those thoughts to myself because I didn't want to deflate my balloon of hope too soon; that would be too much that day. Instead, we scheduled appointments and MRIs in Calgary every four months for the next year to track the progress. I also received strict instructions on what to document: weight loss/gain, moods, medications and how she was reacting to them. And they made it crystal clear that if Kimberley needed any medical attention by a general practitioner, the clinic must be called immediately. The only doctors who were allowed to change the cocktail of meds they put Kim on were the doctors at the Movement Disorders Clinic. She was not allowed to take herself off them, which had been a problem already. She said she felt better and concluded that she didn't need them anymore, which was both dangerous and scary. This crucial fact was imprinted in my mind, and I hoped I could reiterate it to my family with the intensity it was delivered to me.

I collected my belongings when I was stopped one last time by the doctor's words.

"Diana, we will do our very best to ensure Kimberley has good care, but you must understand that this situation is dire. I hope one day we get a name, but we cannot do that until your mom passes."

There it was, the conversation I'd been avoiding.

"Diana, you may want to consider donating your mother's brain to us so we can study it. It's our only hope in getting somewhere with this illness."

The strange perplexity of emotions mixed up inside me created a queasy rumble in my low belly. With it, a deep knowing emerged that my only chance to help my sister laid in my living mother, the answers to this illness locked within her deteriorated brain. I stared blankly at my blue purse. I was lost; in over my head.

"You can have some time to think about this, Diana. Discuss it with your family. We have a very good neuropathology team that are the finest experts in the field. If we can see where the brain atrophies, we may find some commonalities with other people and unlock some mysteries surrounding this illness. I wish we could get more information on the living brain, but the truth is, the brain is too complex for even science to get an exact read on things to see what is happening. There are many areas that wire together, so dissecting it will tell us the story your mother never could."

With that, I knew I needed to tell the family the plan of donating mother's brain to science so we could make an advancement in illnesses like this. Maybe that would give Kimberley the fighting chance she needed. In the cruel way the world worked, I needed to lose my mother for a chance to save my sister.

Chapter 52

Who Cares?

Back home in our apartment in St. Brieux, the world seemed quieter. I was alone with my thoughts too much, which fostered doubt and chronic overthinking of decisions around Kim's health. My days were filled with work, and during my breaks I arranged caregiver funding because I had to face the fact that even if someone would do it for free, they shouldn't have to. The province of Saskatchewan approved me to hire someone, but I'd learned that government doesn't work quickly. On April 7, I was still waiting on the final paperwork I submitted in January.

Trudy had been taking care of Kim for a few months, and they seemed to get along. I sensed the tension at times; taking care of a full-grown woman who isn't related to you isn't an easy job. Sometimes I forgot Trudy was there for Dad; they were together and she was thrown into caregiving, a role she wasn't expecting when they started dating.

I received weekly reports, mostly from Dad. As the disease ravaged Kim's slight body and broke down her mind, the familiarity of this mystery illness crept in. The calling cards shuffling feet, slurred speech and wetting herself were the things other people noticed, but the scope of areas this disease affected were endless. It took away everything she had and left her empty. I would say broken, but when the brain atrophies, the cells die and become waste, so there is nothing there. That is what the doctors meant when they said, "Her brain is shrinking." Quite literally, it is. She may have had one neuron firing off to a part of the brain that had completely disappeared, so what remained was disjointed parts and pieces which could no longer fire or wire together. It was the tragic reality of a broken mind and scattered neurons. The soul, however, was still well intact and visible through the blank stares that greeted me in my sister's steel blue eyes. These same eyes had haunted me over my lifetime. These windows to the soul looked empty of life but held my gaze. I patiently waited for them to share the answers only they held.

"Diana, we have a situation, but I need you sit down." Aaron's voice slid through the phone gently into my ear like it used to when I was having an asthma attack; calm, soothing, yet I knew the situation was grave.

My instincts heightened as I sank into the green fabric couch, which was cool to my skin on an unseasonably crisp mid-April evening. Our sleek black cordless phone was pressed hard against my ear. My heart quickened as Aaron's voice tried to settle me from afar.

"We can't find Kim. Trudy has taken her," Aaron said, dropping the facts on my lap.

I melted into the couch and panic robbed my voice.

"We are trying to see if Chris has any leads. Dad is a wreck. Honestly, Diana, I don't know many details, only that she isn't here, Trudy is gone, and we have to find her!"

He was doing his best to be strong for me, I could feel it, but nothing but panic and worry coursed through our veins as I burst into tears. As my mind caught up with what he said, I jumped up and paced the house.

"Did you call the cops? I need to come home! Did you call Chris? What happened? Where is Dad?"

The questions launched from my mouth landing on the other end of the phone in front of Aaron. As I paced, Aaron reiterated the few details he knew.

"Let's wait and see if Chris can track her down. I was at work; Dad was in the shop. He and Trudy had a fight, and she mentioned something about going back home, but she doesn't have a place to live. Remember, Chris is dating her daughter [complicated, I know], so I hope he will find out what's going on. It's going to be OK, Diana."

Holding back tears was impossible, so the dam broke as I fell to my knees at the mercy of the world and gravity.

"How much more can we take, Aaron? How much more? Kim has some money, is Trudy after that? Why would she take her? Why didn't she just ask? We could have sorted something out! Now she is God knows where, doing God knows what with someone we thought we could trust! I'm going to have to take care of her, Aaron! This is such a mess!"

Fear dominated my mind, and all rationale went out the window.

"Diana, if Chris can't find out what's going on, then we can notify the police, but until then we have to get off the phone in case he is trying to reach us. Let's sit tight. I know this is hard, but we have to dig deep here, Diana, stay calm and get through it. I promise we are doing everything we can to find her."

I could hear Dad moaning, "Oh God," in the background, which snapped me back from my panic. I needed to be strong for him. I could not add fuel to our fire.

"OK, so this is the plan: It's 6:30, I will start packing. If I don't hear from you by ten tonight I will come down first thing in the morning and you will call the police. Thoughts? I mean I want to come down, but maybe I should stay put just on the off chance they come this way?"

"Yes, OK, solid plan," Aaron said. "Alright, so we should free up the phone line in case Chris is trying to call. I will keep in touch, and as soon as I know anything, I'll let you know, OK? It's gonna be OK."

Aaron reassured me, as he had my entire life.

Brent and I waited, rather impatiently, packing to distract ourselves. Moments of panic overcame me as I walked to the phone to check the dial tone every couple of minutes. Patience had never been my strong suit, and it was being tested to the max. At 9:50, I could no longer handle it, so I asked Brent to load up the car. I wanted to call Lindsay but knew I couldn't tie up the phone line. I was just about to pick up the phone to call Aaron and tell him we were on our way when it rang.

"Diana, we found her!" his words boomed over the line.

My knees buckled so I grabbed the end table to stabilize my body. My brain signalled relief.

"Where? When? What happened? Why? Is she home?"

I couldn't contain my relief or joy she was found!

"She isn't home yet, but she will be tomorrow," Aaron said excitedly. "She's in Edmonton with Trudy, Chris tracked them down, thank God! Trudy was upset with Dad and decided to visit her family and take Kim with her. Kim is good, she will be home tomorrow. Trudy and Dad are done, obviously. She will pack up her stuff, but now we really need someone to take care of Kim. Dad is going to call Wes' ex and see if she could do something for us. Have we heard back from individualized funding?"

"Wow, that was a lot to take in...she's OK?" I stammered through tears.

"Yes, she's OK. We are almost through this sick situation. We just need that funding lined up."

"Yes, I know. I'll call. We should be close to signing the papers. If Jessica will take care of her for now, that is best. Kim knows and likes her. At this point, I kind of want people we know and are close with the family to do this job. Our trust has been broken, and I am nervous to allow someone else in. Ugh, I hate this, I can't do the job. When I mentioned it to Kim, she went right to a frown. Not going to happen. She has a boundary set when it comes to us, and I respect that. But we have to figure this out because THIS situation cannot happen again!"

We both knew it, even though I said it. None of us could take this, and Kim deserved someone we could all trust.

Chapter 53

Brave Enough

Much of my time after that was consumed with securing funding and hiring two people to share the difficult job of caregiving. I had never done payroll, so I didn't know what I was doing. Money in our family was always tainted with the idea it is bad, so, naturally, I was not very good with this aspect of Kim's care. The system had me overwhelmed with deductions and accountability, and I was even worse at mailing the cheques. Being four hours away added more challenges to this, so I was barely keeping my head above water and felt this whole situation was going to sink me. I had just turned twenty-five and should have been focused on paying down my student loans, and building a career and family. Instead, I was desperately trying to hold tight to the smallest life preserver in the world.

As I dealt with everything this illness encompassed, I found an idle mind was my foe. In efforts to keep my emotions from getting the better of me, I threw myself into everything else that I had some control over and tried not to think of the painful guilt that was knocking at my door.

Sometimes, I closed my eyes and pictured Kim well, my mind wandering into a daydream of her living on a farm, tending animals. She was married and became a mother to a few children. She was laughing, happy. This was always how I'd pictured her life, simple and full at the same time. I'd live down the road, also married with children. We'd spend time together, raise our children together. Cousins would have sleepovers while we shared a drink on the porch and watched them grow and play. We'd reminisce about our childhoods and help each other come to terms with the trauma. We'd miss our mother together. We'd face our father together. We'd do life together. All I wanted was to have my sister by my side each and every day.

Silence sat between Kimberley and I as the illness took greater hold. There were notable changes each day; her brain was failing her, and I was trying not to fail her, our father, our family as well. I was trying not to fail Brent as his fiancé who was supposed to be planning a wedding. I was trying not to fail at work. In actuality, the person I was failing the most was me. I didn't notice, but my people pleasing, fixing tendencies had gained full control over my life. I never once asked myself what I needed or wanted. Questions like that were for people with options, something I did not have.

Asking Kim how she feels about this seemed impossible. The thoughts were stuck in my head like mud. I couldn't see how to form my fears and pain into questions or conversations with Kim. It was in the silence where painful moments mostly took place, so talking filled the emptiness. The silence allowed the illness to creep inside, stealing voices. Silence equated fear, and I suppose my silence when wanting to talk about this with Kim meant I was afraid, but of what? The answers to those scary questions sat in my brain. Did I really want to know how it felt to know exactly what your future held? No one knows what the future will bring unless you're Kim. She knows. She should be free to cry and talk and share all her thoughts with me, her best friend. But our thoughts remained jailed.

Sometimes I danced around the subject, hoping we might happen upon a natural conversation before the guard throws away the key, keeping her voice, her thoughts, locked away forever. We never did. Perhaps that was how it was meant to be—the answers didn't need to be said. In typical non-verbal communication fashion, I knew the answers. I didn't need the words to confirm what the heart and soul felt. It was how I'd lived my life one feeling at a time. Words filled the silence, but the senses still picked up on all forms of communications, verbal and non. This is the gift of the illness silently said.